Lord, Te

1

Lord, Teach us to Pray

. . . the Lord's Prayer explored and applied

John Belham

Parva Press

Published by Parva Press
P.O. Box 67
DEREHAM,
NR20 4TY, England

First published 2000 by Parva Press.

British Library Cataloguing in Publication Data.
A catalogue record for this book is available from the British Library.

ISBN 0 9537489 0 1

The scripture quotations, paraphrases and allusions are taken from the Holy Bible Authorized King James Version.

Printed and bound in Great Britain by
Morris Printing, Norwich.

To the glory of God
and for the encouragement of his people.

Acknowledgments . . .

Many years back Dr J. I. Packer wrote a series of short articles on the Lord's Prayer for inclusion in church magazines. It was this series that first began to open my eyes to the richness, breadth and depth of this most wonderful of prayers. I gladly and gratefully acknowledge that all that follows has sprung from those early seeds.

I would also like to acknowledge the help of Mrs Beryl Leveridge who patiently turned spidery scribbles into typescript, Mr Mike Ebbens for his computer expertise, Trevor and Jennifer Handel and family members for the artwork and the help of all those who have commented on the emerging manuscript.

Contents

Our Father in heaven,
Hallowed be your name.
Your kingdom come.
Your will be done in earth, as it is in heaven.
Give us this day our daily bread.
And forgive us our debts, as we forgive our debtors.
And lead us not into temptation,
but deliver us from evil:
For yours is the kingdom, and the power,
and the glory for ever, Amen.

An invitation . . .

You are personally invited to spend time at one of the great royal houses. You are to be welcomed as an honoured guest and given complete freedom to enjoy the magnificence of the state rooms, but also to have freedom to visit the more practical rooms - the kitchens, store-rooms, even the bathrooms and security-rooms - to be free to meet members of the household, to admire the furnishings, to pause at the windows and enjoy both the lovely gardens and the great, sweeping views across the estate.

Such, and infinitely greater, is the magnificent invitation given to every disciple within the lines of the Lord's Prayer. Rather than a prayer to be repeated, it is more like a magnificent house to explore.

As with a great house, childishness might lead us to rush from room to room without any appreciation of the privilege of the invitation or of the beauty of the rooms and their setting. We would all too soon find it boring. And, sadly, many true Christian folk find the Lord's Prayer to be just that.

However, given patience and a willingness to apply it to each part of our personal and social life, we will be thrilled to discover what a manual for Christian living is contained in these few memorable words.

For those who will accept it with wonder and a humble willingness to learn, the Lord's Prayer is an invitation to be greatly treasured. It will move us to trust, challenge us to give and stir us to worship. It will show us the depths of our unforgiving hearts and teach us to walk warily. Above all, it will open our eyes to see what it is to live with the single aim of bringing glory to our heavenly Father.

10

Our Father in heaven
... the gracious encounter

The Lord's Prayer is recorded in the gospels of both Matthew and Luke. In Matthew it is part of the teaching in the Sermon on the Mount concerning godly giving, praying and fasting. In Luke it is a response to the disciples' request to teach them to pray. Jesus would have taught the great matters of faith on several occasions and in different situations, and so there is no great difficulty in making allowance for the differences between the two accounts we have.

According to Luke's account, the disciples had been with Jesus for many months. They had heard him speak and seen him heal the sick and set men free. They had also seen their Lord rise a great while before daybreak to be quiet; to spend time alone with his heavenly Father.

Luke tells us that Jesus had just returned from such a time of prayer, and so it was natural for them to ask, 'Lord, teach us to pray.' As a result of that request we have what we call 'The Lord's Prayer'. The prayer is our Lord's teaching and our Lord's pattern concerning prayer. It is how we should pray.

The Lord's Prayer was not given as a literary masterpiece to be viewed and admired. Nor is it a beautiful set piece to be recited morning by morning as if the lovely words would infuse a beauty into our lives but had no practical meaning or bearing on the way we live. It was given to be a pattern and basis of prayer for real people in the real world. It is the pattern our Lord has given his disciples. Even then it is not simply a recitation or a set prayer but truly a whole house of prayer with many rooms to explore. Each room opens to us a different aspect of God's world, the world for which we are called to pray.

Beware then, of rushing around the house from room to room simply 'checking them off'. But rather, take time to walk from room to room and bring before our heavenly Father, the people, the contents and the views, both near and far, of each room in turn.

We begin with just the first phrase, 'Our Father in heaven,' or, 'Father,' as it is in the earliest copies of Luke's gospel. Here is the grand entrance hall in which we are introduced to the King. Our Lord teaches us straight away to whom we should pray and, indeed, who may pray in this way.

To whom should we pray?

Our Lord was teaching his Hebrew disciples to pray, and the Hebrew people were very proud of Abraham their father. Abraham was the friend of God. Abraham was successful in pleading with God to spare cities. It would have been quite natural, from their point of view at least, for our Lord to have taught them to pray: 'Father Abraham, friend of God, plead for us, pray for us.' But he did not do that.

There were other great spiritual leaders, for example Moses. When God spoke to ordinary men, he spoke to them from a distance, but when God spoke with Moses he spoke with him face to face. So it would have been natural, again from the disciples' point of view, if our Lord had said, 'Pray like this: "Father Moses to whom has been given the privilege of speaking with God face to face, pray for us, intercede for us, pray on our behalf."' But again, he did not. The same of Elijah, that great man of God by whose passionate prayers came drought, fire and rain: 'Elijah pray for us, intercede on our behalf.'

Our Lord nowhere teaches us to pray in this way, and there is an enormous lesson here straight away. If we would be disciples of our Lord Jesus, and are willing to submit to his teaching, we will not offer our prayers to those Old Testament saints or to their New Testament counterparts.

There are many servants of God to whom church people have been encouraged to pray: St. Jude, St. Mary and other spiritual giants of scripture and those who have followed them throughout the centuries of church history. It is clearly right to learn all we can from the wisdom and lives of the great servants of God. But can it be right to pray to them or through them? Although for some it is very painful, it must be said that this is not our Lord's pattern. In this prayer our Lord offers us a privilege far, far greater. We are not invited to come to a mere servant of God, no matter how great a spiritual giant he or she may have been. We are invited to come with boldness into the very presence of the God and Father of our Lord Jesus Christ; invited to speak with Almighty God himself.

The invitation is absolutely overwhelming. How dare we? We certainly may not by any merit or right of our own. But, through his Son, the Lord God invites us, as we pray, to come into his awesome and royal presence; indeed, we are called to do so with boldness, and by express invitation.

Once we have understood the greatness and amazing privilege of such an invitation, to refuse would be as unthinkably rude as receiving an invitation to a royal reception or garden party but, on the occasion, actively choosing to speak only with the servants.

How should we address Almighty God?

Then further, we are taught to approach Almighty God as 'our Father in heaven'. This again is something absolutely wonderful; that we, mere mortals, are invited to address the sovereign Lord of all the universe as 'Father'. The Hebrew people of our Lord's day knew almost nothing of this intimate knowledge of God. And in our own day and culture, for a variety of reasons, many people find it very difficult. We think more easily of God as an impersonal cosmic force, or maybe the pattern set by our own father is a great stumbling block. However, the privilege of Christ's disciples is that we may know God, the Sovereign Lord, as our heavenly Father; the best and greatest of Fathers, who loves and cares for us.

The apostle Paul puts it even more strongly when he says that those who have the Spirit of our Lord Jesus can address God the creator as 'Abba', 'Father, my Father'. That is the privilege of disciples of our Lord Jesus. We can, in a real sense, be sons and daughters with the freedom of approach seen in a little child with a loving parent. We are taught to come with boldness to the creator King, our heavenly Father who loves us, longs for the very best for us and provides for our every need.

Who may pray like this?
Here is a prayer for disciples of our Lord Jesus. He came to his own people, writes the apostle John, and they did not receive him. They rejected him. But to those among them who received him he gave the power, the right, the authority to be the sons and daughters of God.

Those in our own day who are given this right and privilege, are also those who receive the Lord Jesus; those who are willing to trust him for who he is and for what he has done; willing to learn what he commands and willing to do it. These, and only these, are the true disciples of Christ and to them is given this great and glorious privilege . . . to be the sons and daughters of God.

The family prayer
Finally, do notice that the prayer begins with the little word *our*, not just *my Father* but *our Father*. The one who hears equally the cries of the strong man or the little child, the prince in his palace or the poor man cast out. He, our Father, hears the cry of the prisoner as clearly as the cry of the free, the prayers of the despised as gladly as the prayers of those held in high public esteem.

True disciples of the Lord Jesus, no matter what their earthly circumstances, are no more, and no less, than sons and daughters of the living God and are invited to come with equal boldness, and with equal humility, as brothers and sisters into the very presence of God. The squire and the stable hand, the president and the plumber, the carpenter and the king, disciples met behind cottage doors or cathedral doors – 'our Father'.

Here truly is common prayer, a prayer common to disciples from every nation, tongue and tribe, a prayer for the smallest child and a prayer for the strongest leader, a prayer for those who have the responsibility of great wealth and for fellow disciples who do not even know whether there will be a next meal.

When we truly begin to grasp that our fellow disciples, no matter what their earthly circumstances may be, are our brothers and sisters in Christ, it will begin to move our hearts with God-like compassion as it challenges us to give and forgive, to share and to care for those around us.

In beginning to pray the Lord's Prayer, pray just this first line, 'Our Father in heaven,' and then, before moving on, think about it. Pause and reflect into whose presence we are invited to come with such boldness. Step back and in wonder reflect that we may speak with the Lord God himself. Recall at what cost that privilege was bought; reflect with the apostle Paul that, 'The Son of God loved me and gave himself for me.'

If you pause and consider these things you may well be moved to worship, and moved in wonder and love for God who gave his only Son for you. Filled with awe and wonder, prayer begins to come alive; prayer to our Father in heaven who cares passionately about this world and its people; who cares enough about us to make us his children.

'Father, give us a due sense of awe and wonder at the greatness of this your invitation. Set our hearts ablaze in wonder and thanksgiving that in your unchanging love and mercy you gave your Son, your only Son, that we, together, might be sons and daughters of the living God.'

References
> *Given in the order in which they occur in the chapter.*

The Lord's Prayer - Matthew 6:5-14
The Lord's Prayer - Luke 11:1-4
Abraham pleading - Genesis 18:22-33
Moses speaking face to face - Exodus 33:9-11
Elijah, passionate prayer - James 5:17&18
God as 'Abba' - Romans 8:14-17
The right to be the sons and daughters of God - John 1:11&12
We love him, because he first loved us - 1 John 4:19

Questions
> *These questions are offered simply as an optional help to personal study and group discussion.*

1 How do you respond to the suggestion that the Lord's Prayer is more than a prayer to recite; it is also a prayer to explore and apply phrase by phrase?

2 In the light of the fact that so many church people have been encouraged to pray to saints, do you find it rather surprising that our Lord did not teach us to pray to or through the great servants of God?

3 How would you feel about someone attending a royal garden party and choosing to speak only to the servants?

4 Can you sense the wonder of the privilege of addressing almighty God as 'Father'?

5 Who can rightly do so?

6 How can this move us to worship and bring our prayers to life?

7 What is the significance of the little word *our*?

Hallowed be your name
... worship,
but not only with our lips

From the grand entrance hall our Lord leads us into the first of the three great state rooms which lie at the heart of this royal house.

Like a great house, the Lord's Prayer is built around three magnificent central rooms. They are a passionate concern for the honour of our heavenly Father's name, the extending of his kingdom and the doing of his will. These three great concerns lie at the heart of the prayer and must surely be the concerns of all those who are true disciples.

As the text comes to us in the Greek, each of these first three petitions is short, God-centred, urgent and complete, 'Hallow your name, Bring in your kingdom, Cause your will to be done . . .' The words reflect and inspire an eagerness to see God's sovereign rule completely and finally established. They look forward to the fulfilment of human history but they also fire our personal thinking and touch our individual lives here and now.

Beginning in this chapter with just the first of these petitions, when we pray, 'Hallowed be thy name,' or, 'May your name be honoured,' what do we mean? We know the line so well and recite it so easily, and yet do we really appreciate the weight and significance of these simple words?

Three questions may help to show the richness of their meaning: Firstly . . . Why should we want to see our heavenly Father's name honoured?

Whose is the name we should long to see held in awe? It is not the bare word 'God' itself, used too easily when people find that they have forgotten something they needed, or hit their thumb with a hammer! Nor are we taught to honour a god of our own picturing, such as 'the God of love' or 'the great designer.' Rather, we are taught to honour the name of the God and Father of our Lord Jesus Christ, the king of the universe whose character is revealed in scripture. He is the great 'I am' who is and always will be Lord and redeemer.

i) . . .He brought us into existence, loves and cares for us.
In biblical shorthand, our heavenly Father is maker or creator of the whole universe. Such an understanding does not bind us to any narrow or rigid human theory but does affirm that our heavenly Father is author of all and Lord of all. Our seemingly godless world - with all its exploitation and suffering - is still in his hands. He is in control of nations, governments and societies. On a personal level, our circumstances, our life, our future, this next week, are all in his hands. Whether we choose to acknowledge it or not, he is the one who has our very breath in his hand. Should not then his name be honoured and held in awe?

ii) . . . We are answerable to him.
As author and maker our heavenly Father has every right to determine how we, his creatures, should behave. Through his chosen spokesmen he has given us very full guidelines for living. He has also warned us that he will call us to account for the life he has entrusted to us. The Bible describes him as judge. Our words and our deeds, both open and secret, good and evil, are known to him. We shall be called to account for those evil things which we deliberately do and also for that steady rebellion which just ignores him, chooses not to do his will and so fails to honour him. The charge laid before Belshazzar, the ancient king of Babylon, on the night of his death was simply this, 'The God in whose hand is your breath, and all your ways, you have failed to honour.'

iii) . . . At great cost he made possible our rescue.
The Lord is the creator, the judge and also, wonderfully, our redeemer . . . our heavenly Father cares about this world, cares about each one of us, enough to pay the price for our rescue. He gave his Son so that those who believe will not be swept away in judgment and banished from his heaven, but might each be made acceptable before him, given a fresh new start and made a child of God. Here and now his redeemed people have this vital relationship with their heavenly Father; a relationship that not even death can snatch away; they have life everlasting.

God is the creator, the judge and the saviour. Should not his wonderful name be held high, honoured?
In Stuart Hine's words:

> *Then sings my soul, my Saviour God, to Thee,*
> *How great Thou art!   How great Thou art!*

Of course, if it can be proved that God is in no sense author or creator, then it follows that he has no right to tell us how to live or to call us to account for the style of life we choose. It also follows that there is no need of a rescuer or redeemer to put us right with him. Hence the great assault by godless men on the concept of God as creator. However, despite our unthinking or wilful turning our back on God, our heavenly Father remains on the throne. He is creator, judge and redeemer and it is fundamental to our well-being that his name be held high, honoured.

So to the second question . . . What does it mean to 'hallow' or 'honour' the name of our heavenly Father?

If we do not have a high regard for people who live or work in the same place as ourselves, we simply take no notice of them. If we are considering our career or marriage, or even just planning a holiday we would not dream of consulting them. We are just not interested in their opinion, let alone their advice or moral judgment. If we do not honour someone, in this sense of holding them in esteem, we do not have to say anything or do anything, we simply pass them by. We ignore them: neighbour, teacher, husband, wife, work colleague, or parent. We ignore them because we regard their opinion and their advice as irrelevant. In practice, many of us behave just like this towards God. We ignore him, we fail to honour the God in whose hand is our very breath.

On the other hand, if we have a high regard for someone, when we are considering something, if we are able to, we consult them. We will say, 'Now I wonder what so-and-so would think about this?' or, 'I wonder what so-and-so would do in this situation?' This is how we honour them and this is how we should honour our heavenly Father. As we come to make great decisions, we should ask, 'I wonder what the Lord God has caused to be written about this?' 'Is there some plain teaching, some instruction, a principle or a warning in the scriptures that would apply to this situation?' This is how to honour him and hold high his name; it involves love, respect and, above all, a longing to please him in all that we do and say.

Naturally enough, if we hold his name in such esteem we will not tread it underfoot in our everyday conversation and habits of speech. We will not use it cheaply as a swear-word or expletive nor enjoy hearing others doing so. Rather, it will be natural to tell out the greatness of God and to bring honour to his name by our whole way of speaking and living. How well the proverb puts it, 'Give me neither great wealth nor poverty, lest in wealth I forget you, or in poverty I am driven to steal and so bring dishonour on your name.' We honour or dishonour our heavenly Father not only with our lips, by what we say, but with our entire way of life.

The old word was *magnify*, used in the original Latin sense of *showing forth the magnificence* of God. In other words, 'Let his name be seen and heard to be magnificent, as it truly is.' So to honour his name, to hallow it, means to hold it in such awe that those around may both see in our lives and hear from our lips the greatness of our heavenly Father.

Which leads us to ask thirdly . . . How and where should his name be honoured?

i) . . . Honoured in our world

'Let all the world in every corner sing, "My God and King,"' wrote George Herbert. This world's peace ultimately depends on the extent to which our heavenly Father's name is honoured. Here is a call to pray that his name may be honoured throughout the whole world and in particular by its statesmen and leaders. Disciples of the Lord Jesus are called to pray and work that his name might be honoured in the corridors of power. If world leaders and peoples share a common submission to our heavenly Father there is a strong foundation for peace and understanding. Pray that God's name might indeed be hallowed by the great leaders and nations of this world.

ii) . . . Honoured in our own land.

The scriptures teach that it is godly living or 'righteousness' that exalts a nation. It is when our Father's name is honoured that a nation becomes truly great. Historically, there is a very striking link between Britain's standing among the nations and our national concern for the things of God. Look for yourself and see the link, historical evidence of the fulfilment of the promise of God. Why? Because, if you have God-fearing men and women in positions of authority and leadership, there will be just laws and fair dealing both nationally and internationally. Study the history of the founding of what is now the United States of America and see this same principle at work. When our Father's name is honoured individuals are valued, the weak are protected, evil, violence and vice are restrained and all that is good is encouraged and supported. These are God's purposes for those in authority or government at every level from parliament to our own homes. Such world-changing thinking lies at the heart of the Lord's Prayer and it is brought most sharply into focus as we pray, 'Your will be done.'

iii) . . . Honoured in the church at large.
What is the church? It is intended to be God's own people, called out to live for him. A people who will honour him in the way they speak and in the way they live. But the church in Britain, although holding the form of religion, seems chiefly concerned with self-preservation and ceremony and has largely forgotten this radical call to live totally for God, to seek first the honour of his name. We need to pray that our Father's name might be honoured in his Church, nationally.

iv) . . . Honoured in our own local churches.
Locally, we have a great museum very close to the church. Our prayer and determination is that the church building, although it is far more ancient than the museum, may not become a 'museum of Christianity'. We long that it might be the meeting place of a vital community of people who love God, and who live, speak and care in such a way as to be a strength, an encouragement and a challenge to those around us; a community of people who truly bring honour to the name of our heavenly Father.

And, finally, v) . . . Honoured in our own lives.
If we really pray the Lord's Prayer, our prayers will affect the world, our nation and our church, and they will also profoundly affect our own homes and lives. We shall begin to pray, 'Lord God may your name be honoured in my own home, in my own working life, in the way I speak, in the way I behave, in my relationships with those around me.'

These are the areas in our own lives on which we need to reflect as we pray, 'Hallowed be your name.'

As you consider this phrase in the Lord's Prayer, reflect on the day that lies ahead, the people you will meet, those who you naturally like and those who provoke you and whose every word seems calculated to trip you, annoy you or crush you with criticism. 'Lord, you know how my blood pressure rises - may your name be honoured . . .' .

Helmut Thielicke, the great German pastor and preacher, tells of a businessman who, moving from file to file or interview to interview, would pause just for a moment between each task, take a deep breath and say, 'Glory be to the Father, the Son and the Holy Spirit, Amen,' and then press on. What was he doing? He was really praying, 'May your name be honoured as I tackle this, or as I see this person.' We need to learn to follow his example. Even as we sit down to write a letter – 'May your name be honoured,' 'Glory be to . . .'

We are only at the first line! Yet if you would in any way begin to plumb the incredible depth of this prayer, pause, consider and apply the words to the world in which we live and then cry from the heart, 'Hallowed be your name.'

'Lord, teach us to pray, may indeed our Father's great name be held high and honoured in our world, in our country, in our own lives and in the lives of those we love.'

References
'The judge of all the earth' - Genesis 18:23-25
'God in whose hand is our breath' - Daniel 5:22&23
The Lord our Redeemer - Galatians 4:4&5, John 3:16 etc.
'Give me not great wealth or poverty' - Proverbs 30:8&9
'O magnify the Lord with me' - Psalm 34:3
Righteousness and greatness - Proverbs 14:34

Questions
1 What three great concerns are said to be the three great 'state rooms' of this prayer? Should they be the chief concerns of each true disciple?

2 Why should our heavenly Father's name be held in awe and in the highest honour?

3 How can we hold his name high?

4 Can you think of a situation where someone has been ignored, treated as if they were not there or did not count?

5 Do we do this to Almighty God?

6 How natural and easy is it to remember the Lord as we make our daily decisions?

7 How does stealing bring dishonour to the name of our heavenly Father? Would cheating, tax evasion, drunkenness or reckless driving do the same?

Your kingdom come
... the king and his domain

By royal invitation we move into the second of the three great state rooms of this prayer, 'Your kingdom come.'

On a personal level, on entering this awesome throne room, we do well if we find ourselves holding our breath, walking on tip-toe, overwhelmed by the sheer magnificence of the one in whose hand is our breath. Like the noble and godly prophet Isaiah of old, in the presence of the glory of God, we find ourselves unworthy, undone and totally dependent upon his mercy.

In our own over-casual society, we need to be reminded of the awesome holiness of God. The very nature of our heavenly Father, the one to whom we are invited to pray demands, not a cheery greeting but a bended knee, a lowered face . . . and wonder.

Here in this great state room we are brought face to face with the glory of the Lord; he is the King of Kings. The whole universe is his, he is Lord over all beings, good and evil, heavenly and earthly. The very existence of earth's proud empires is in his hand and he laughs at the little human schemes that challenge his sovereignty. The whole earth is the Lord's, to him belongs all power and glory and majesty.

Why then, if the kingdom of God is so great, are we taught to pray for the coming of his kingdom? To him every knee shall bow but until that day, from a fallen world, a world in rebellion, our heavenly Father is calling out a people who will turn and gladly, freely and willingly submit to his kingly rule. By the willing submission of his subjects, God, the rightful Lord, has chosen to re-establish his kingdom on earth. It is both for that glorious final day and for this free and voluntary turning to God that disciples are called to pray.

The kingdom of God is variously described in the New Testament as, 'The kingdom of heaven,' 'The kingdom of God,' 'The kingdom of Christ and of God,' 'The kingdom of his beloved Son' and in Revelation as 'The kingdom of our Lord and of his Christ.' We are called to pray that this kingdom may come, but called to pray not in terms of armies and crusades, not in terms of conquests, not, indeed, in terms of human rule or territory at all. For the kingdom of God is not of this world. It is a kingdom that leaps every kind of human boundary; it cannot be contained by prison bars or chains, it cannot be excluded by iron or bamboo curtains, political or religious barriers. It is not at all like the passing and territorial kingdoms and empires of this world. It is, rather, like seed growing in each nation. In some societies it flourishes, in others it is crushed, in some it all but withers away. There have been seasons in British history when the kingdom of God has grown, thrived and been fruitful beyond measure. But in our own day widespread secular thinking, the pursuit of pleasure and the drive for material gain have all but choked it.

Where is the kingdom of heaven to be found?

Firstly, the kingdom comes here on earth where God the Father and his Son, the Lord Jesus, are honoured. As Jesus came to his own people, he said, 'The kingdom of God is among you.' He is the gateway, the door of the kingdom, he is the source of our forgiveness and wholeness. As people came and honoured him, so they became members of the kingdom. Zacchaeus, a hated tax collector for the occupying Roman overlords, was a man whose life was totally changed as he honoured the Lord; salvation came to his house. The kingdom came there. Or Nicodemus, the teacher and leader, who came to Jesus at night secretly searching for the truth; the kingdom comes when men like Nicodemus or Zacchaeus come and, as Jesus put it, are 'born over again' or 'born from above' by the Holy Spirit. Such people are born of God; they are changed by being made a new creation. The kingdom of God is within them, within their individual lives.

Wherever God's kingdom or rule is found, there will be totally changed people; people who will live for God; people who know the Lord Jesus for who he is; people in whose lives God the Holy Spirit has taken up residence. The kingdom of heaven is the joyful acceptance of the rule of God within our individual lives. It is a kingdom of grace and forgiveness, giving us a fresh new start as a disciple of Christ, as a child of God and as a citizen of the kingdom of heaven. The kingdom touches us one by one and, through our changed lives, touches our homes, the affairs of those around us and ultimately the affairs of cities and nations.

Then, secondly, the kingdom of heaven is found among disciples as they meet together locally. It may be in great congregations or in tiny house groups. Jesus said, 'Where two or three are met in my name, I will be there.' So, when we meet to pray together as brothers and sisters in Christ and to work together for the kingdom of heaven, Jesus promised that he, by his Holy Spirit, would be with us binding us together and giving a common mind. For example, in 19th century England a small group of wealthy and influential men met in Clapham to pray and encourage one another in bringing about godly social change. They worked towards the abolition of slavery abroad, and the provision of hospitals, education and better working conditions for the less well-off in this country.

In a very different setting, in Germany, when Adolph Hitler and the Nazis were rising to power and crushing anyone who might resist them, little groups of Christians met to pray and encourage each other. There was the kingdom; the kingdom that would stand when the Third Reich had long since gone. Such little groups are typical of the kingdom of God under oppression.

Thirdly, the kingdom of heaven is among his people right across the world. From every nation, language and tribe God, by his Holy Spirit, is calling out a people for himself. Although our circumstances and cultures differ very greatly, it is thrilling to discover ourselves brothers and sisters in Christ, fellow citizens of his kingdom.

Finally, fourthly and supremely, the kingdom will come when the Lord Jesus returns. Then every knee will bow. At present the Lord Jesus, his kingdom and his people can be sneered at, ignored and forgotten by the world at large. But that will not be so when he returns. To him has been given all authority. He will return, not this time in humility, but with great power and glory as King of Kings and as judge of all people. He will return, and then the kingdom will be plainly seen. Then the King and his people will be recognised for who they are: Jesus the Lord of Lords, the One to whom every knee shall bow, and those most to be envied among human kind, those on whom our heavenly Father has set his love, the children of the kingdom, the sons and daughters of the living God.

'Till he comes,' is a constant refrain of the scriptures. We are to watch and pray; we are to be about our Father's business; we are to keep faith, we are to hold fast, 'till he comes.' That phrase should ring in our hearts and minds as the motivation for all we do and think.

Here, then, is the kingdom as it touches this world. It is where Jesus is honoured in individual lives, among his people both locally and internationally and when he returns in glory.

In practice, how should we pray, 'Your kingdom come'?

The petition is very practical, for under this heading should come all our prayers concerning the shaping of our own lives; all our prayers for our loved ones and family; all our prayers for the people with whom we mix day by day at work, at leisure and in our local community. Only then, can we look out and catch the magnificent vision of our town, our country, our world won for the kingdom of God.

Every great house has its particular places from which can be seen the most magnificent views. Views not only over the formal gardens and estate but sweeping on and over woodland, farmland and maybe out to sea. Such is the view given to us as we pray, 'Your kingdom come.'

The Great Commission to bring the gospel to the world is here in the phrase, 'Your kingdom come.' Here is the true heart of all mission and outreach. How then should we pray for missionaries of the gospel wherever they may be? What should be the content of our prayers? Pray, certainly, for their provision and safety and for God's overruling hand on their circumstances - all the subjects of this great prayer - but supremely, pray that our Father's kingdom may come:

- Pray that as they speak and seek to be alongside people, men and women, boys and girls may be touched by the Holy Spirit of God; that the Lord's presence and glory may be known amongst that people.

- Pray that as they train, teach and encourage local Christians, the kingdom may come.

Here, within these few words, is the whole true aim of missionary work; that the kingdom of heaven may come to embrace every nation. It includes both the great sweep of prayer for the whole world and also specific prayer for individual missionaries known to us in their particular need.

Taught a prayer like this, and given the Great Commission to go into all the world, every true disciple will be involved in missionary work either directly, by going and sharing the gospel, or indirectly by supporting those who have gone on our behalf. We cannot truly pray, 'May your kingdom come,' without it touching the way in which we live, our career, our prayer life and how we use our money. As we pray for those who have gone out to preach the gospel, pray for their safety, usefulness and well-being, but pray above all that the Holy Spirit may use them, that God's kingdom may come.

I shall never forget the impact of the words of a Kenyan pastor who, on coming to this country, was at pains to thank us as a people for sending out our finest sons and daughters to bring the gospel to Kenya some fifty years before. How far would the bringing of the kingdom of God to an unknown and perhaps dangerous people feature in our hopes and ambitions for ourselves and for our children?

We need to pray that God's kingdom would come in our own land, too. We live in a land where, by and large, people have turned away from God, regard him as irrelevant. Pray, therefore, for spiritual revival; that we may turn again to him. Pray that God would raise up and strengthen godly leaders in the church, in politics, medicine, education and in every area of our national life. Men of God in times past set up industries on clear, godly principles. For example the Frys and the Cadburys, the chocolate manufacturers, very deliberately set out to run their businesses with godly, Christian integrity. That is why we have places like Bournville, a 'garden village', because its founders were profoundly concerned with the well-being of their people, not just with 'cash flow'.

In Britain we have a church that appears to be dying. Pray that God would revive his church and raise up those who will relevantly teach what the apostles taught. Pray that across our nation he will give people a spiritual hunger. The disciples were accused of filling Jerusalem with their teaching. May our cities and towns also be filled with faithful, godly teaching. Jesus taught that the kingdom of heaven is to a society as yeast is to bread. We need to pray that our society, too, may be permeated by men, women and youngsters living for God.

Our churches, chapels and meeting places are so often seen as relics of the past, irrelevant to today's world. But our buildings should be places where God's kingdom is seen at its very best and from which it grows in every community; places where the Lord is present among his people in a very special way as they meet to worship, pray, learn of him and encourage one another. Pray that our Father's lordship may be seen in our dealings with one another. Pray that men and women and young people might bow the knee to the Lord Jesus. Here is the grand purpose of fellowship groups, Sunday schools and youngsters' clubs - not just for friendship or entertainment but for the kingdom of God. Pray that each group might be touched by relevant, godly teaching and godly thinking. Do we share this longing, this great concern that God's kingdom might come where we live? That the Lord God might touch lives, by his Holy Spirit, in and through our local church?

Finally, and least comfortably, as we pray, 'Your kingdom come,' we do well to pause and think about our own lives. 'Lord God show me where I stand before you, that I might not deceive myself, or wear a mask before others.'

In this great state room, if we have eyes to see the kingdom at all, we immediately find ourselves unmasked and unworthy. We are challenged to examine ourselves to see if we are truly part of the kingdom; challenged, also, to see if the rule of God is touching and permeating every part of our lives. We must begin here for then, and only then, shall we be increasingly able to play our part for the kingdom from our own homes to the ends of the earth. We are called to be the answer to our own prayer, to bring each part of our lives under the rule of God, and then to pray, work and encourage those around us, wherever God our heavenly Father puts us, to bow the knee to the King of Kings.

We tend to put our lives in little packets, little compartments, all kept separately. The slot on Sunday morning or evening may well be 'very godly', but our heavenly Father wants us to be a people of integrity, all of a piece. Not just Sunday, but Saturday night and Monday morning; business, pleasure and worship all brought under his rule. It is too easy to pray on Sunday, defraud on Monday, deceive on Tuesday . . . . . God looks for integrity, his kingdom and his rule touching every part of our lives; true godliness of living in our work and in our leisure.

It is very interesting to see how we tend to think of whole areas of our life as being quite outside God's concern, areas that we couldn't possibly pray about or ask for the Holy Spirit's guiding or control. For example, anger, resentment or our family relationships; or maybe, our use of time or handling of money; our sex life, ambitions or career. But should this be so? If we are truly disciples of Christ should we not be able to pray about each and every part of our lives and say, 'Lord, I want to please you, honour you, by your grace may your kingdom come in this part of my life'?

Here is a very practical prayer. 'Your kingdom come.' Pause and pray, letting your prayers move from God's purpose for each part of your own life, to his purposes for the community, the land and the world. 'May your kingdom come.'

Your kingdom come

In this simple petition our Lord inspires the question that every true disciple needs, constantly, to be asking: 'What would my Father have me to do for his kingdom? What part can I play? What gifts has my heavenly Father given me to help build, strengthen or establish his kingdom locally, nationally, internationally?' Here, in so short a phrase, is the whole purpose of life! 'Your kingdom come.'

'Father, we thank you, again, for your mercy towards us. In thankfulness may we honour you, not only with our lips, but in our lives. Hasten the day when your kingdom comes in every department of our own lives, in our homes, churches, cities and throughout your lovely, but rebellious world, for the glory of your great and holy name.'

References

Isaiah before God - Isaiah 6:1-5
'Power and glory and majesty' - 1 Chronicles 29:11
'The kingdom of heaven' - Matthew 3:2, 4:17,10:7
'The kingdom of God' - Matthew 6:33
'The kingdom of Christ and of God' - Ephesians 5:5
'The kingdom of his beloved Son' - Colossians 1:3
'Not of this world' - John 18:36
'The kingdom among you' - Luke 17:21
Jesus, the door of the kingdom - John 10:9
Zacchaeus - Luke 19:1-10
Nicodemus - John 3:1-8
'A new creation' - 2 Corinthians 5:17
'Two or three in my name' - Matthew 18:20
'From every nation, language and tribe' - Revelation 5:9
'Until he comes' - 1 Corinthians 11:26
'Watch and pray' - Mark 13:32-37
'In power and glory' - Mark 13:26 & 14:62
'Every knee shall bow' - Philippians 2:5-11
The Great Commission - Matthew 28:19&20

Questions

1 In our culture have we lost the perspective of the awesomeness of God our heavenly Father? Are we more likely to approach him with a cheery greeting than with awe and wonder?

2 How has our heavenly Father chosen to re-establish his rule on earth? Could it be coloured on an atlas as an empire?

3 Can you think of someone you know whose life has been totally changed by the coming of the kingdom of heaven?
In what local group, known to you, can the kingdom of heaven be found?
In what way will the kingdom eventually touch every nation?

4 At present the kingdom of God can be ignored or sneered at - will it always be so?

5 Why should, 'Your kingdom come,' be most important in our praying for our friends and family?

6 How can such a simple petition be at the heart of all missionary and outreach work?

7 'We cannot truly pray, "Your kingdom come," without it touching the way we live, our career, our prayer life, and the way we use our money.' Is this true? If it is, are we truly praying it?

8 Is the grand purpose of our local church, its groups and young people's work, friendship and wholesome entertainment or the kingdom of heaven?

9 How easy is it to packet parts of our own life quite separately? Would we admit to having areas of life that we have yet to bring under the rule of Christ?

10 Does Christian maturity lie in the direction of being disciples in every area of our lives, of being all of a piece, consistently Christian?

Your will be done
. . . godly living and dying

As we are led into the last of the three great state rooms of this royal house of prayer, we find ourselves in an awesome and holy place, a place where we come face to face with both the ecstasy and the anguish of true godliness, a place where heaven touches earth: 'Your will be done on earth as it is in heaven.'

As if the rooms were linked by great double doors, this petition is all of a piece with the one before it: 'Your kingdom come.' It is found in the early texts of Matthew's gospel and some of those of Luke, and is an outworking of the same principle: that God's rule may be seen as we live in practical obedience to our heavenly Father's instructions and guidance.

How then shall we pray it? How should we apply it to the great sweep of human activity here on earth and also to our own particular circumstances and concerns? We can make this petition on many levels: personally, locally, nationally and internationally. It is a very spacious room and from its windows we can look out and pray for those we love, our church and community, our land and our world. The great scenes of prayer are all here: 'Your will be done.' But, first and most pointedly, the challenge is to apply it to our own lives.

It is a prayer with both an active and a passive side. Actively, we are called to pray for God's overruling hand on the affairs of this world, that his will may be done. Actively, we are challenged to pursue all that is in accordance with his will in our own lives and in the lives of those for whom we are responsible. Passively, we are called to accept what is his will, even when it is to our own personal discomfort or even anguish.

In heaven our Father's will is done gladly, willingly, completely and joyfully - may it be like that on earth. May there be a foretaste, a 'touch of heaven' about our lives, our decisions and our communities here and now under the pressures and in the cut and thrust of earthly living.

Firstly, personally and actively: 'Your will be done. May the way I live, all that I do and say be pleasing before you.'

The Lord is our pattern, he did as he taught. This petition is not just, 'Do what I teach.' He did it, lived it and fulfilled it: 'My meat, my essential food, my first priority is to do the will of him who sent me.' What he said, he said as from the Father. What he did, he did to please his Father.

Here, then, is the all-embracing prayer for those who would follow the Lord Jesus, for those who really want to love God with all their heart, mind and strength.

It is a prayer for every stage of life. When we are young it is our parents who make the decisions. So parents might well pray, 'May your will be done as we bring up these little ones, teaching them love, discipline and right from wrong.' As we get older we start thinking for ourselves about, for example, schools and particular subjects for study and so youngsters and parents begin to share the decisions. 'May your will be done, may your guiding hand be on our thinking.'

With growing independence, 'Your will be done,' will work itself out in prayers like these:

'May my relationships with the world around me be honouring before you.'

'May I view its resources as a trust to be valued, used and handed on, rather than to be selfishly exploited, polluted and destroyed.'

'May my treatment of animals be kind.'

'Show me the deep and hidden prejudices of my heart so that my treatment of my fellow human beings from different groups and cultures may be fair and just and pleasing before you.'

'May I constantly seek to use my days as you would wish me to.'

'May my work be done in a way that pleases you.'

'Your will be done, today - even Monday morning! - at work, at college, at home.'

Work and money, love, sex, marriage, family life and leisure, attitudes to the world and people around us, they are all here!

'Father, may we learn your right way and live in a way that pleases you.'

In the light of scripture, with its warnings, instructions and commands, this petition, 'Your will be done,' enables us to examine ourselves. It is like one of the great wall mirrors so characteristic of stately homes. Here, as it were, is a mirror in which we can see ourselves as God our heavenly Father sees us. As we look we are brought face to face with a reflection that challenges us and gives us an opportunity to put right each part of our lives before him.

Secondly, our Father's will for our lives accepted - the passive aspect of this prayer.

What a marvellous but terrifying pattern was set by the three Old Testament friends of Daniel. As a public test of loyalty to the state, we read that they were required to fall down and worship Nebuchadnezzar's great statue. Although they were the king's loyal subjects, in utter loyalty to the Lord God they were willing to face even death rather than offer such false worship. Their response to the king has much to teach us:

'Our God is able to deliver us from the furnace, and we believe he will, but if not, let it be known to you that we will not serve your gods or worship the golden image.'

The three short words, 'But if not,' tell us that their stand was no mere fleeting act of rash bravado but a terrifyingly courageous submission to the will of God, to whom they had pledged their total loyalty. 'But if not,' words echoed by the Lord himself in the garden of Gethsemane as he faced the double agony of the cross. He knew full well that his Father was able to save him from that hour, yet he prayed, 'Nevertheless, your will be done.' As he looked ahead to the agony of the cross, our Lord taught his disciples to pray, 'Your will be done on earth as it is in heaven.' To do his Father's will was his constant aim and joy, as it can be for us, but in Gethsemane it was his agony, his passion.

Jesus knowingly set his face to go to Jerusalem. Events did not overtake him, he was not swept by overwhelming circumstances to his death. He came, as he had said, to do his Father's will. From the beginning he had accepted that this would mean his death. On several occasions he had taken the disciples aside to warn them of it, and yet humanly he shrank from it. 'Father, if this cup can pass,' - the agony and the anguish of it - 'let it pass, but if not, may your will be done.' Our Lord accepted his Father's will, submitted to it, despite the suffering.

Locally, we have been called as a church to pray for a whole series of very sick people, called to pray that God in his mercy would restore them to health. In praying that his will be done we have needed to be ready to accept what comes from the hand of our loving heavenly Father, be it life and health or sickness and death.

Humanly, the Lord Jesus shrank from the cross. Humanly, we would hold on to those whom we love. How hard a lesson to learn: 'Nevertheless, your will be done.'

John Calvin as he lay dying said: 'You are slaying me, Lord, yet it is enough for me to know that it is your hand that is slaying me.' Here is the way to pray, passively, 'Your will be done.' For even through sickness and in death we can bring honour to his name.

If we begin to pray it with understanding, we will find this great state room of the Lord's Prayer distinctly challenging and uncomfortable. It has within it a great reforming principle which, if really worked out rather than just repeated, will change our thinking, speaking and way of living. It will begin to make us Christ-like, holy.

'Heavenly Father may we not only hear the beautiful words of this prayer, but follow them, obey them, shape our living and our dying around them.'

References
'My meat is to do the will' - John 4:34
'Our God is able' - Daniel 3:16&17
'Nevertheless, your will be done' - Luke 22:39-42

Questions
1 What is meant by the active and the passive sides to this petition?

2 In what sense is the petition, 'Your will be done,' the all embracing prayer for disciples?

3 In what ways does the petition touch our everyday living?

4 How hard is it to accept the will of our heavenly Father when it is not to our comfort or to the comfort of those we love?

5 How much is the petition, 'Your will be done,' reflected in our Lord's own life, ministry and death?

6 To what extent should this petition shape our own living and dying?

Your will be done continued
. . . the great principle
of godly government

As we look at this great petition, we must begin and end with personal holiness of living, living a life that is worthy of the gospel. And yet, perhaps, like a guest in a great house, caught and challenged by our reflection in a great mirror we move rapidly out of its range to the comfort of a great window where we can look out on the world. The view is far less personal and far less threatening!

Clearly, in heaven God's will is done willingly, gladly and joyfully. May it be like that upon earth. May our national and international policies, laws and treaties be godly. May they have about them a touch of heaven.

The apostle Paul urges us to pray widely and especially for kings and those in authority. When we hear that leaders of great nations are meeting to work out treaties, to hammer out understandings, or to work out a common approach to a rising evil – we are to pray. We are to pray that the Lord's will might be done; that the agreements might be just and based on honesty and integrity and that they might be pleasing before him.

Our heavenly Father is able to overrule the activities of quite unbelieving men and women. In the Old Testament we read of Cyrus, who cared nothing for God, and yet he was God's chosen instrument. It is not Washington, Beijing, Moscow nor any other human power centre that is in ultimate control. It is the Sovereign Lord who is in control. As Nebuchadnezzar had so painfully to learn, 'The Most High God rules in the affairs of mankind.' He is God; he reigns.

We are called to pray, 'Your will be done, knowingly or unknowingly, in international affairs.' Read the newspapers, watch the TV and pray, 'Your will be done on earth.'

We live in a fallen world where, from time to time, men and women with fearful ambitions will arise to crush and conquer those around them. We are only safe when the godly are most mighty. We are only safe when the greatest power is in the hands of godly people and godly nations. Only then can wild and destructive men be restrained. Only then can we live in safety, for, although they may make many mistakes, godly men and women can be trusted to use their power against an oppressor and trusted also not to use it for aggression, ambition, or greed.

Thank God for the peace we enjoy and pray for godly government and godly ways at every level of society. For on God, and on his good hand on all those entrusted with authority, depends the well-being of our nation and, indeed, of our world.

Thomas Cranmer and his fellow compilers, with brilliant spiritual insight, taught us to pray for those in high government office just along these lines. He taught us to pray that they might faithfully and impartially administer justice for the restraining of all that is evil or corrupting and for the support and encouragement of all that is godly and excellent.

That they may truly and indifferently minister justice to the punishment of wickedness and vice and to the maintenance of true religion and virtue.

The old words sound hard in our day, and yet they carry the seed of all that it means to really pray, 'Your will be done,' throughout every level of society.

Modern thinking concerning government is that it should always be morally neutral, not adjusting punishments and rewards to restrain evil and corruption and promote the good and godly, but simply to provide the necessary support to enable its citizens to enjoy a free choice of lifestyle, godly or ungodly, moral or corrupt. As a direct result of abandoning the biblical perspective of the God-given privilege and responsibility of government, well intentioned modern governments actually find themselves presiding over the moral collapse of society.

We need to recapture the biblical perspective so beautifully taught in these few words; words from the prayer for the church in the 1662 Prayer Book - a prayer all but forgotten by the modern church.

It takes some unpacking because both the language and the times have changed. The little word 'truly' carries with it the biblical understanding that those set in any position of authority are answerable to God for their decisions and actions. They are not free agents in a position of power by chance, there to deliver their own opinions and do what they will. They are agents of God, put in that position of authority to look after the best interests of those for whom they are responsible. Here is a prayer that those placed by God in any position of authority might discharge that responsibility faithfully before him.

When we use the word 'indifferent' we mean we do not care either way about some matter. But in Cranmer's day it meant even-handedness, showing no difference between rich and poor, strong and weak as justice is administered. It is a prayer for fairness, impartiality and equity. And rightly so, for always the temptation is to be partial; to have one kind of justice for the prince and quite another for the pauper. The temptation is to caution the well-spoken driver of an expensive car and fine the leather-clad motor cyclist. There is great pressure to take note, as we are wined and dined, of the skilful presentation of the powerful business concern and overlook the simple letter of an ordinary person who is being crushed or abused by that concern in its pursuit of financial gain.

Here is a prayer that those appointed to administer justice might do so impartially before God.

'To the punishment of wickedness and vice.' That sounds harsh to our ears, and perhaps 'punishment' is too narrow. However, one purpose of government is to restrain evil; to associate some kind of high cost with wrong doing and so make evil more difficult to practise. This can certainly be done by fining or locking people up. But it can also be done by the passing of laws which so balance the rewards as to make it less desirable to practise life styles that would, directly or indirectly, wreck or undermine society. Here is a great principle of government: to restrain evil.

And vice? Vice is all that would corrupt and break down our society, all that would undermine godly living. The words 'vice' and 'corruption' have almost lost their meaning in our tolerant but ungodly society where all kinds of morality and immorality are accepted side by side.

In our pursuit of individual, adult freedom are we not increasingly in danger of failing to protect vulnerable groups? We have, for example, all but removed legal protection for the unborn child. We are in danger of repealing laws that would protect young people from sexual exploitation. And by allowing parenting partnerships to become so casual, we have exposed a great many young people to abuse either in the home or, as they flee from it, on the streets. Those in high places are called to restrain those who would exploit others and to protect the vulnerable.

'And to the maintenance of true religion and virtue.' There is a negative, restraining role of government and there is also the positive maintaining and supporting role, the helping forward of everything that is truly good and godly. Not, notice, necessarily the support of great church schemes and structures but rather the maintaining of true faith and godliness among the people.

The role of government is also the support and encouragement of all that is good and excellent, noble and true in society. It is to support and help forward the best, for example, of business practice, medical practice and educational practice as well as to support the best in social practice and family life.

There are godly members in our Parliament who realise that the traditional family is under great pressure, is penalised by our tax and benefit laws. They are concerned about it because it undermines society, so they work and speak to put this right. Thank God for such men and women.

'Your will be done in terms of our national laws.'

But it comes closer to home than this, for most of us will find ourselves, at one time or another, in some kind of position of authority where we must 'govern' in the broad sense of this word. We govern as we play our part as a parent, committee member, teacher, leader, shop-steward or manager. In each situation we are called to be faithful and impartial, to cast our vote and to do all in our power to restrain evil and promote good and godly ways.

So finally, to the root and source of the whole matter: 'Your will be done in our own lives.' We begin and end here because, frankly, this is the most difficult - to actually govern our own public and private lives before God determined to restrain evil and to pursue everything godly and good. How can we play our proper part before God in our family, church, society or nation until we begin to govern ourselves?

King George VI was one day quietly asked if he was one of the Lord's people, and His Majesty willingly answered for both himself and his Queen to the effect that they did indeed honour the Lord and sought to shape their way of living by his word. There was the King graciously confessing the faith. What a King! Here is the key question; could we, too, confess that faith? For here, within ourselves is the primary battle. Only by the grace of God can we begin to live a life that pleases him, or even wish to do so.

The Ten Commandments, brushed aside in our own day, have been given to tell us the things that God hates in order that we may recognise them and, by his grace, restrain ourselves. God calls us to restrain ourselves from idolatry, theft, murder, adultery and from that envy of other people's privileges, possessions or power that is coveting. A tendency towards these things comes all too easily and naturally to us. The commandments have been given to show us what our heavenly Father longs to see. They are given in order that we may recognise our failure and turn to live in a way that pleases him. If we would 'govern' ourselves before him we must learn to restrain the evil in our own lives and to pursue all that is godly, noble, excellent and worthy of following.

These things are basic. As we begin to put these things right before our heavenly Father then, imperfect though we are, we can begin to step out and play our part for the honour of his name at every level of society; parent, manager, statesman or monarch.

Are we willing, faithfully and impartially before God, to play our part? Are we willing to stand against all that is evil; all that would undermine or corrupt, and to promote and support all that is godly, honourable and excellent? Are we willing for his holy ways to control our own living and speaking: at home, at leisure and in our business, social and political lives? Do we really want his will to be done on earth as it is in heaven?

The Lord's Prayer is perhaps not the charming prayer we thought it was! Whatever our position in society, it is an invitation to walk in very uncomfortable places!

'Father, grant us wisdom and courage to stand for you. May "your will be done" not only by our passive acceptance of your will but also by our active standing against evil, and by our pursuing of all that would bring glory to your name and of all that would further the well-being of those around us.'

References

Pray for kings and those in authority – 1 Timothy 2 :1&2
Cyrus, God's servant - Isaiah 45:1-6
'The Most High God rules' - Daniel 4:24&25

Questions

1 How important is it for disciples to read the newspapers or watch the news and pray, 'Your will be done'?

2 What lesson did Nebuchadnezzar have to learn?

3 'We are only safe when the godly are most mighty.' What happens when evil people are most mighty: a) in the household, b) in the classroom, c) in the neighbourhood, d) in the courts of law, e) in the nation, f) in the world?

4 Do modern governments pass laws that steadily restrain evil and promote good?

5 Can you think of groups of vulnerable people who need to be protected by law?

6 If a government aims to maintain godliness is there a distinction to be drawn between upholding 'church institutions' and promoting true godliness of living? (Could this have been the basis the clash between the scribes and pharisees and Jesus?)

7 Can rewards and penalties be rightly used to encourage good and godly ways?

8 There are many levels at which we can be given authority, called to 'govern' - from looking after a younger brother for half an hour to being a world statesman. At what levels of 'government' are we personally involved? Can the principles set out in this chapter be applied to each level?

9 It is not popular to think of governing and restraining ourselves. However, do disciples of Christ need to recognise their weaknesses and by the grace of God be restrained gossips, thieves, cheats, liars, adulterers etc.? For by nature are we not capable of such things?

As it is in heaven
. . . a shaft of sunlight

'Thy will be done,' stern and glorious, yet through an open doorway in this great state room we catch a glimpse of a glorious, colourful, sunlit conservatory or garden room, a glimpse of what is yet to be; a glimpse of heaven. And beyond that heart-stirring glimpse lies heaven itself, the whole garden; a place of incredible beauty and peace; a place where we can walk at ease with our heavenly Father. 'Today,' said our Lord to the penitent thief, 'you will be with me in Paradise.' Paradise is the garden of God.

The Lord teaches us to pray that our heavenly Father's will might be done here, on earth, as it is done in heaven. Here, we long to see God's name honoured and yet see it so often trodden under foot. We long to see God's kingdom come and yet see the fulfilment of our prayers so often frustrated or long delayed. We long to see eyes opened and hearts set on fire for God, and yet see them dulled and blinded by preoccupation with wealth, pleasure and care. We long to see God's will done and yet find a clash of wills, our own as well as the determined will of godless folk around us. Here, we pray, live and battle that the glory of heaven might be seen. There, it is seen in all its fullness.

For our encouragement and strengthening our Lord turns our eyes and thoughts heavenward where his name is honoured, where his kingdom is complete and where his will is done perfectly, willingly and with joy. He teaches us to pray, 'Father, may it be like that on earth.' He gives us hope. He gives us a note of praise. He lifts our eyes, in the middle of the prayer, to catch the wonder of heaven - where our heavenly Father is, and where his will is perfectly done. This heavenly note is there to stir, challenge and refresh us as we pray. It is a moment of praise, a shaft of sunlight, a turning of our eyes away from the struggles of earth to the glory of heaven.

We are very much rooted and grounded in this present world. It is very hard to think of heaven, and yet the Bible, throughout, is very 'heavenly minded'. It is constantly reminding us that our citizenship is not here, but in heaven.

Where is heaven? When the astronauts of the former USSR first broke free from this earth's atmosphere, they took the opportunity to score a point for atheism by declaring from space that there was neither God nor heaven to be seen. And yet, they really only shot down an 'Aunt Sally'. They destroyed a false picture. God, who inhabits eternity, is outside of time and space. We have not broken out of time and space by breaking free of this earth's atmosphere. That is, relatively, only a small step. God is outside of the whole universe which is all part of time and space. Heaven is a different realm; eternity, where God is, is not limited by time or space.

Another very basic question is: Who will be there? Matthew begins the prayer with the phrase, 'Our Father in heaven.' God, our heavenly Father, is there. He is there, says the apostle John, with the Lamb, the Lord Jesus. Together they share the throne and around the throne are innumerable heavenly beings who do his will gladly, willingly and joyfully.

Destined to join them - and this is awesome, wonderful and almost beyond our comprehension - mere human beings like ourselves. This is our heavenly Father's great purpose on earth. He is calling out men, women and young people from every nation and tribe to be his own people here and now and ultimately to be with him, where he is, in heaven. Disciples have a destiny, says the New Testament, to rule over angels who are themselves the very messengers of God.

Who will be there? Sadly, there are those who will not be there. For where God is, in his very presence, there will be nothing ungodly, unholy, or impure. In the light of this, who can stand accepted before God? The very disturbing fact is that not one of us has a natural ticket for heaven. Our only hope is in God our heavenly Father who of his mercy has made it possible for us to be made perfect and acceptable before him. Here lies the heart of the Christian message. It is God's amnesty for fallen men and women, an acceptability before God that is not our own but given to us - given to us at the price of the cross of the Lord from heaven.

It is those who respond to our Father's mercy in the Lord Jesus who will be there in heaven. It will be those to whom he has given the right to be his sons and daughters. The mark, the guarantee of those who are citizens of heaven is the Holy Spirit of God at work within us; opening our eyes to see the kingdom of God, bringing us into that kingdom, enabling us to live for God and changing us little by little into Christ-like people.

In Charles Wesley's words:

> *Changed from glory into glory,*
> *Till in heaven we take our place.*

This process of being changed is the Holy Spirit's marvellous work in the life of a disciple. A changed life, an increasingly godly life, is evidence of the Holy Spirit's work and is the seal of our citizenship of heaven. Of course, the opposite also applies. Religious interest or religious talk without changed habits of living, stand as a terrible warning sign.

We all want to be citizens of heaven. The other place, the alternative, is to be shut out from our Father's presence and is at all costs to be avoided. It is described in scripture only in the most terrible terms of suffering and loss, ruin and endless regret. It is described in terms of men and women, loved and made in the image of God, yet who have turned their back on God or lived in this world as if they were not answerable to him. By doing so, they have missed their true destiny and calling to be the sons and daughters of our heavenly Father, citizens of heaven.

How do the apostles speak of heaven?

'I heard a voice from heaven,' writes St. John, 'saying to me, "Write this: From now on blessed, happy are those who die in the Lord."' Those who die 'in the Lord', who die in true faith, are happy, are blessed. And we will never feel the force of that word 'blessed' until we say 'how much to be envied' are those who die in the Lord. They are most to be envied because they are God's own people destined to be with him where he is.

As disciples we are children of earth, and yet our true citizenship is not here but in heaven. We pass our time here as pilgrims, but we are passing through. It is for this reason that we must not bind ourselves too closely with the things of this world. We are here about our Father's business but our destiny is to be with our Father in heaven, to be with our Lord, to be with the saints in glory. We will take our place at the great feast, in the fellowship, the oneness, the unity of love, understanding and purpose that is heaven. There, not here, is our home! The apostle Paul was torn as he wrote to the church at Philippi, he wanted to continue to encourage them and yet he longed 'to be with Christ which is far better.'

Once we have grasped such a picture of heaven, we will see why 'to die in Christ' is of all things most to be envied. When we truly see it, it will directly affect the way we live here and now. It will affect our living and it will affect our dying. It will affect the way in which we come to view the dying of our loved ones. It is always terribly hard to let them go. When a loved one dies we are shattered, torn apart. God has set us in families and among friends with bonds of love and companionship that are so strong that in grief we are left absolutely desolate. And yet, if we have really taken hold of the fact that it is so enviable, such joy, to be with Christ; that it is a journey completed, a race run, that our loved ones in Christ have now reached home, then, surely, there is no greater comfort for those of us who are left. It is right to weep, our loss is terrible, but not for them, for they are at home with the Lord. They are safely in his hands. The Lord has taken them to be with him where he is.

Such a grasp of heaven will also affect our approach to our own last day. Of course we are built, as human beings, to hold on strongly; to live. And yet if we really have, as the apostle Paul had, an understanding of heaven, a real longing to be with Christ, an assurance of a welcome home by the mercy of God, then there will come a time when we know that there is no longer need to cling on to this life; a time when it becomes right to put ourselves in his hands to take us home. We can look forward to being with the Lord.

Visiting Tom, a man in a Manchester hospital, the conversation turned to heaven. Tom was dying and knew it. He was only expected to live a few days. Suddenly, Tom was praying, putting into his heavenly Father's hands his own departure. It was very wonderful. Something of the glory and wonder of heaven shone through that prayer. It was unforgettable. Here was a man ready, prepared. He knew that to be with Christ was far better and he longed to be there. He, too, was torn with loved ones at hand and yet he knew that his time had come and that to be with the Lord was far better.

Heaven. Take hold of it strongly. To be with the Lord is far better. When it comes to the day of dying, those who die in the Lord are most to be envied.

The apostle John tells us that heaven is the place of freedom, freedom from oppression, freedom from suffering. Tom himself had suffered much, as so many do, disabled and living with pain. Now he was on the doorstep of freedom from the suffering that had been his lot in this life. We are mortal and we live in a fallen world where sickness and suffering form the backcloth of our human existence, particularly in our closing years. By God's grace the science of medicine can help us marvellously. Given grace to accept our situation, we can rise above suffering with great courage and patience. Sometimes, by the goodness of God, there is physical healing here and now. But the ultimate victory, complete freedom, is not found here but in heaven.

Again, in this life the world presses hard, sometimes very hard indeed. We have fellow disciples even now hounded, threatened, persecuted or shut up in prisons and labour camps under oppressive, atheistic or fanatically religious regimes. There are many occasions in both Old and New Testaments which speak of godly people and how, on occasion, the ungodly will hate them and deliberately delight in crushing them and pouring scorn on their faith. We may be scorned and ill treated here but in heaven the world can no longer cause us to suffer, we will be free, there will be no more tears.

Here on earth we are dogged with weaknesses and with great temptations. Paul, too, knew the weakness of the flesh. 'The things I long to do, I fail to do and the things I long not to do, I find myself doing.' That is the nature of this earthly life. But in heaven - freedom. And freedom, also, from the limitations of this earthly body, from the limitations of time and space. Here there are things that we long to do, but because of our personal limitations or circumstances just cannot do. There, we will be able to do his will with perfect freedom.

Then in heaven there will be rest. The apostle John writes, 'They rest from their labours.' John was almost certainly for a time a slave labourer in the mines of the prison island of Patmos. He knew about the sweat and toil of this earth. John encourages us to think of heaven, not in sentimental terms of floating about on clouds playing harps(!), but as our Lord taught us to think about it in this prayer. It is a place of freedom from pressure, a place of creative rest and exhilarating activity, where God's will is done perfectly, gladly and joyfully. This is worship in the fullest sense. There will be singing, but not just singing. It will be singing coupled with service as we are freely about our Father's business. His will done perfectly, in heaven.

Then there will be joy. 'In your presence,' says the Psalmist, 'there is fullness of joy.' We will be 'with the Lord', and with those whom we have loved and lost awhile. We will understand then with new insight all that has passed. Here we wrestle in a fallen world with many hurts and hardships; there we shall see, as has been so well put, the beautiful side of the tapestry of life. Here we struggle, seeing only the ends and agonised knots; there, will be joy, fullness of joy, the joy of home.

Here, we run a race. Here, we fight a battle. There, in heaven, is laid up an inheritance, a reward, a joy, a homecoming, and most prized and glorious of all, the crowning words of the Lord Jesus Christ, 'Well done, good and faithful servant, enter into the joy of your Lord.'

Sing then, from the heart, with John Newton,

> *Let the world deride or pity*   (. . .For it will!)
> *I will glory in thy name.*
> *. . . Solid joys and lasting treasure*
> *None but Zion's children know.*

'Father, in our tears and battles, lift us, we pray, in hope and in praise to see the glory of heaven. Show us afresh that our citizenship, and the citizenship of all those on whom you have set your love, is not here but with yourself in heaven.'

References
Paradise - Luke 23:43
Citizenship in heaven - Philippians 3:20
The throne of God and of the Lamb - Revelation 22:3
'From every nation' - Revelation 5:9&10
A destiny to rule over angels - 1 Corinthians 6:3
'Blessed . . . are those who die in the Lord' - Revelation 14:13
'To be with Christ' - Philippians 1:22&23
Hated, 'for my name's sake'- Matthew 24:9, Matthew 5:10-12
       See also, Apocrypha, Wisdom of Solomon 2
'The things I long to do' - Romans 7:15
'They rest from their labours' - Revelation 14:13
'Fullness of joy' - Psalm 16:11
'With the Lord' - 1 Thessalonians 4:17 & Philippians 1:23
A race, a fight and a crown – 2 Timothy 4:7&8
'Enter into the joy of your Lord' - Matthew 25:21&23

Questions

1 Our heavenly Father's will done on earth in the way in which it is done in heaven. To what extent does that thrill and inspire you?

2 Does our culture, interest or position lead us to naturally assume that we have a 'ticket for heaven'? Should we assume it?

3 What is the trustworthy seal or guarantee of our citizenship of heaven?

4 Should and does the picture of the loss and ruin and endless regret of men and women having missed their true destiny fill you with horror? Does it motivate you to action as it did so many of the great missionary pioneers?

5 God's own people are most to be envied. Why?

6 How will a firm hold of the disciple's citizenship of heaven affect our living, our dying and our reaction to the deaths of those we love?

7 'Sickness and suffering form the backcloth of our human existence.' Hard though such a statement is, does it help us to understand our world and our circumstances and help us to ask, 'Why *not* me?' rather than, 'Why me?'

8 Do we care as we should for those who suffer because they are disciples of Christ?

9 We know so little about heaven, but do the New Testament references to homecoming, rest, joy, freedom and 'well done' encourage and strengthen us to face the battles of earth?

Give us today our daily bread
... strength and freedom to live

The honour of our heavenly Father's name, the coming of his kingdom and his will done on earth as it is in heaven. These form the three magnificent state rooms of this great house of prayer. They set the vision, goal and aim for all the more obviously practical petitions that follow.

The petitions for daily bread, a forgiving spirit and spiritual safety do not stand on their own any more than a cluster of kitchens, cloakrooms, store rooms and security rooms would be built in the place of a great house at the centre of a royal estate! The kitchens and cloakrooms are only there to make possible the banquets and royal receptions of the great state rooms, and so it is with this majestic prayer. The petitions concerning our basic needs and safety make it possible for disciples to live freely and wholeheartedly to the glory of God.

We are taught to pray for bread, not just for ourselves and our own comfort, but bread that we might be free from anxious care and so free to live for the glory of our heavenly Father. We are taught to pray for forgiveness and for a willingness to forgive, not to make us 'nice people,' but to enable us to live for the Lord and to work together with one another as a team. And we are taught to pray for safety, again, not for our personal comfort, but rather that we might be able to live as free and faithful servants of the King.

For many of us, however, it is not until we arrive at 'daily bread' that we feel, "Ah, now the prayer really begins. Bread is something that really matters to me. Before it was 'spiritual' and hard to understand, but now we have arrived at 'bread' it really begins to be relevant." Fair enough, but this is only because it meets us where we are, rather than where we ought to be! Having missed the vision of the first three petitions, petitions that lie at the heart of the prayer, we are like the teacher's nightmare of youngsters on an outing to a great house, hurrying through the magnificent state rooms with eyes only for the sweet shop!

Nevertheless, what an encouragement that God our heavenly Father cares about our stomachs. He cares about the things we need day by day; cares about these basic practical details. Samuel Johnson was once challenged about the amount of care he was taking over his stomach. Dr. Johnson replied, 'My dear sir, if I did not take good care of this place I would not be able to take good care of anything else.' It is a fair point, and this is precisely the reason why our Lord taught us to pray, 'Father, give us today our daily bread.'

Here in this petition are the kitchens, store-rooms, provision rooms and accounting rooms of the great house. They are there to keep the table supplied and to make possible the day to day running of the house. They are there to give freedom from anxiety by supplying all that is necessary, 'bread' for today and 'bread' for tomorrow; exactly the thoughts that lie behind this petition. The great difference to note is that our Lord is not talking about the grand and the luxurious but about the simple, basic necessities of life. Our Lord is speaking of physical provision; food to eat, of which bread is the basic example.

If God withholds our daily bread we will be so filled with anxiety about our next meal and where it is coming from, that we will not be able to live seeking first the kingdom of heaven or living for God. We will be completely overwhelmed with anxiety. People are anxious enough should a preacher go on too long and lunch be spoiled! But that is a very different thing from the overwhelming anxiety of actually not knowing where the next meal is coming from or how on earth we are going to escape from an ever spiralling pile of unpaid bills.

Our Lord was concerned that we should not be filled with such anxious care; that we should be able to live before him, as his people, free from this kind of pressure. Therefore, he taught us to pray, 'Give us today our daily bread.'

Bread is a picture and symbol of all that we need physically, mentally and spiritually to live in this world and in this body in a way that brings honour to our heavenly Father.

Our physical needs

Primarily we need food; food both for ourselves and for those who depend on us. At harvest time we acknowledge with the hymn writer Matthias Claudius that:

> *All good gifts around us*
> *Are sent from heaven above.*

Ultimately, all that we need comes by the good hand of God. 'Lord God, thank you for your provision of food, bless those who farm, produce and distribute it and spare us from such poverty or famine that the things of God are forgotten because of our concern for bread.'

But 'daily bread' also includes all our basic human needs, for example shelter and warm clothing. We are taught in this petition to pray, 'Spare us from such poverty, war, civil unrest, lawlessness or family strife that we are forced out of our homes.' These things strike at the very roots of both godly living and of our physical well-being. Family breakdown and strife at home reduces too many in our society to isolated, rootless, homeless, bed and breakfast, bed-sit or cardboard-box dwellers with all the temptations and dangers of exploitation, drugs and sexual abuse. War brutalises us and makes us of necessity killers of our fellow human beings, and in the extreme reduces us to hungry, threadbare refugees all but forced to steal and fight as we compete for food and temporary shelter.

As Hugh Latimer and his fellow reformers preached on 'daily bread' they said something rather surprising. They said, 'When you pray for daily bread, pray first for the government.' Surprising but right, for upon our government, their policies, and God's good hand upon them, will depend whether we have wealth or poverty, enough or too little bread.

Pray that our government may be able to defend us from those who would bring us into subjection, for a subject people are rarely free from poverty. War itself will very quickly consume our wealth and reduce us to being anxious about shelter and food.

Pray, too, that they may be able to maintain justice within our land for if our goods are constantly being stolen or if we are often defrauded then we shall very soon be anxious about daily bread.

Pray, also, for the fair distribution of wealth within society as this is very much a matter of government policy. Unrestrained, market forces will always tend to allow the rich to become richer and the poor to become poorer, which in turn leads to deep resentment and lawlessness. It is a very unfashionable thought, but a large and growing middle income group is a token of good government and a very healthy sign in a society. Whereas the growth of a new super-rich class and of a deprived and increasingly violent underclass is a clear token of government failure.

Pray, too, for those voluntary organisations who, out of compassion, are seeking to alert governments to injustice and to bring help to people whose basic needs are not being met. Pray for our government, that they might have discernment, in the face of the many competing pressure groups, to have an open ear for those who speak for the truly needy and so fulfil their function before God, that each of us might have daily bread.

Pray and thank God for stable, godly government whose task it is to guard and oversee the just provision of our basic human needs. The reformers saw these things clearly and yet it is so up to date! Fresh and modern after 400 years!

Our social and medical needs

Our basic human needs also include mental and physical health. We live in a fallen world where any of us may go through times when we are simply not able to manage; our job collapses, our home life collapses, our health or mental health collapses, our strength fails. Then we need to pray for courage, for practical and medical help, for godly strength to face each day and for a willingness in such circumstances to let go our proud independence and be interdependent as God intended. For God, our heavenly Father, has given us one another, family, friends and the wider society, to provide for each other in our hour of need. In such an hour we are taught to pray for all that we need to face another day in a way that brings honour to our Father in heaven.

Our spiritual needs

Our Lord spent considerable time in prayer and meditation, he did not live by 'bread alone'. We, too, need spiritual nourishment if we are to live as God's people in this world. For example we need opportunity to be alone and quiet before God. We also need an opportunity to read and think about his word, spiritually feeding ourselves day by day. We need the help of godly speakers and writers who can explain God's word to us and help us to shape our thinking and our living to please him. We also need the fellowship, support and encouragement of Christian friends. These things are as basic and necessary as bread.

'Lord, give us a spiritual hunger to know you better, and a longing to serve you more faithfully. Thank you for the spiritual food you provide. Keep us spiritually alive, feeding and growing as disciples day by day.'

We live in a hard world where Christ is shunned and God is forgotten. Pray then for a godly graciousness and for courage. Pray for strength and wisdom to face particular situations. These things, too, are daily bread. We need them fresh day by day if we are going to live as God's people. Day by day, pray: 'Fill me afresh with your Holy Spirit that I might live today in a way that pleases you.' These are prayers for daily bread in the setting of the whole prayer - seeking first our heavenly Father's kingdom and his honour. Put them where they belong! These are not prayers for daily bread for our satisfaction, let alone for our personal comfort or pleasure, they are petitions that we might live for God in his world.

The part that is ours to play

Here, we are in a sense beggars; 'Lord God give us day by day our daily bread.' We are utterly dependent on him, and yet he answers that prayer only in very exceptional circumstances with 'food parcels from heaven.'

There are those who regard it as a mark of being 'spiritual', to choose not to use God's ordinary ways of providing for our daily needs. On this basis they refuse to take ordinary steps to raise money to buy bread, refuse medical help or refuse to prepare when speaking in public. 'The Lord will provide, it shows lack of faith for me to use common sense, use his ordinary provision or play any active part.' Sadly, this is not an uncommon spiritual error, an apparently 'very spiritual' idleness which presumes on the goodness of God. Another great mistake, again abandoning God's ordinary way of providing for our needs, is the passive fatalism which says, 'I choose to do nothing - whatever will be will be - it is the will of God.'

Our heavenly Father's normal way of providing for our daily needs is by the skills he has given us to develop and use, and by sweat and hard work. For this reason true prayer is dangerous! It always has a reforming, life-style changing element in it. We have to be willing to be a part of the answer to our own prayer. We cannot truly pray for bread without being willing to work for it. We will only truly pray for better relationships when we are willing to guard our own tongues, change our own attitudes or control our own behaviour. We will only truly pray for spiritual nourishment and growth when we are willing to set aside time for our heavenly Father and his word and actually allow his word to shape our daily living. We are utterly dependent on God for all that we need; we have also a part to play by self discipline, by skill and by determined hard work.

The farmer prays, 'Lord give us today our daily bread,' and he also farms. We have got to hold these together. We live in a world where our bread, pay packet or salary cheque normally comes by the sweat of our brow. The New Testament teaches that if we wilfully choose not to play our part, we should not eat either!

Oliver Cromwell's advice to his troops was, 'Trust in God . . . and keep your powder dry.' Pray, knowing the outcome depends absolutely on the goodness of God; live, as if it depends absolutely on your own effort. Our very breath is in the hand of our heavenly Father, and yet we have our part to play. Our part is the whole field of scientific discovery and artistic creativity coupled with every part of human skill, understanding, discipline, courage, effort and determination.

'Give us today our daily bread,' does not mean, 'Sit back and watch it fall on our plate.' It calls for all our skill, effort and wisdom *and* humble thankful hearts. Especially humble thankful hearts when, through circumstances beyond our control, we are unable to look after ourselves and are utterly dependent on the goodwill of those around us.

A true commonwealth

Do notice, again, that as our Lord taught us to pray for daily bread he taught us to pray, 'Give *us* today *our* daily bread.' Not just *me* and *my* but *us* and *our*. We are part of a family, part of a society, part of a land and it is together we pray for bread. So, as God gives you bread, remember your brother, your sister who is in need. He feeds *us* together, he gives *us* enough.

As the Reformers considered this they presented a great challenge. It was that those of us to whom God gives plenty are 'God's treasurers'. Our heavenly Father has placed us where we are, in order to help those in need. The good Samaritan of the parable with his donkey, wine and money, 'chanced' to pass that way and find the man in trouble. He was equipped and able to help . . . and he did. As you pray, 'Give us today . . .' and God graciously answers that prayer, don't forget, don't pass by, your neighbour, your fellow disciple who needs your help.

'Why is it,' the visiting British Christian was asked, 'that you Christians in the West have so much while we Christians in the developing countries have so little?' Great trading empires have always amassed wealth at the centre by exploiting those at a distance. We will not truly begin to pray for those with too little bread until it touches our own trading and purchasing practices, the brands we buy, our own pile of bread and our own bank balance. 'Give us today our daily bread . . .' What a marvellous and dangerous prayer! A prayer that threatens our natural complacency, selfishness and greed.

If God is truly *our* Father he is the Father of those who have plenty and the Father of those who are in need. It is all too easy to piously pray, 'O God, feed the starving people of . . .' Real prayers of compassion will always be found to touch our wallet, purse, or cheque book.

George Muller laid his orphanage table though he had nothing to set before his children. As he prayed, so the Lord stirred the hearts of those who had plenty to bring food for the orphanage. Our Father's economy always has two sides, sometimes it is our place to give, and to give generously, and sometimes to receive and to do so humbly and gratefully before God. There is to be a holy interdependence of love and compassion between those who are truly sons and daughters of the living God.

True prayer is life changing. Our heavenly Father is calling out for himself a people who will truly be a commonwealth of individuals, societies and nations. Ungodly self-sufficiency, greed and selfishness will always militate against this, and yet the vision of a true commonwealth lies here, right at the heart of the Lord's prayer.

'Father, thank you for your provision of our daily bread. Thank you for the wealth that we have, personally and as a society. We thank you for stable government and pray for your hand upon it. Help us to use all that you entrust to us in a way that pleases you and awaken us to be fair and generous in our dealings with those who have too little.'

References
Free from anxious care - Matthew 6:25-33
'Bread alone' - Matthew 4:3&4
'Not work, not eat' - 2 Thessalonians 3:10-12
Good Samaritan - Luke 10:33-35

Questions
1 How do you react to the suggestion that we pray these petitions for daily bread, forgiveness and safety, not for our comfort but so that we are free to live for God; free to be about our Father's business?

2 Why do we need to pray for our government as we pray for daily bread?

3 Both nationally and individually we like to think of ourselves as strong and independent 'towers of strength' but are we? Should we be? Can we be, when in the tough situations of life?

4 Do our prayers have a reforming, lifestyle-changing element about them? Are we willing, at our own expense or effort, to be our heavenly Father's answer to our own prayers?

5 How can the petition for daily bread touch and enlighten the selection of the goods we buy?

6 'Real prayers of compassion will always be found to touch our wallet, purse, cheque book and career.' How easy is this? Is it true? Does it happen?

7 The vision of a true commonwealth is right here in the Lord's Prayer, what stops it happening?

Forgive us our trespasses
...a fresh clean start

A humble, though essential, room in any great house is the boot room, a room full of pegs and racks, hats and coats, boots and shoes of every kind and size. Although the great doors will be opened and the carpet rolled out on occasion, this humble boot room is the essential way in for family members.

Near-by will be found a wash room. It may be outside in the courtyard or in the house conveniently placed near the boot room. Together these practical rooms make it possible for household members to be made acceptable in the house.

You enter the house not across velvet lawns, but across real lawns with worm casts and mud. You enter from the mess of the stables or the mud of the estate and these humble rooms are the way in. Here you wash and leave behind your soiled boots and your outer clothing, garb totally unacceptable within the house. It is simply not acceptable to sit at table, on a beautifully embroidered seat, unwashed, in dirty boots, muddy overtrousers and anorak!

Our heavenly Father, too, has made provision for those soiled by the real world in which we live. The rooms are rooms of forgiveness, cleansing and mercy and all true members of the household must pass this way and do so often.

'Forgive us our trespasses as we forgive those who trespass against us.' The forgiveness of little things and the forgiveness of very great things; our Father's forgiveness of us and our forgiveness of others.

In this chapter we look at the first part of the petition; God's forgiveness of us, 'Forgive us our sins, our trespasses.' Such a prayer is basic to our spiritual well-being and standing before God. We must first come to our heavenly Father, as our Lord has taught us, and simply pray, 'Forgive us our trespasses.' What does that actually mean? For the meaning is slightly hidden by the word 'trespasses'. 'Write off and set us free from our total debt', is closer to the Greek. But, even so, what is our debt to God our heavenly Father? What debt do we owe to the One in whose hand is our very breath and to whom we owe our very existence?

- We owe him love. He brought us into being for his pleasure, to give him glory in our lives and to enjoy him for ever. We owe him a debt of love, practically expressed in doing what pleases him.

- We owe him a willingness to refrain from all that would pollute us before him; to steer clear of all that we know to be active disobedience or rebellion against him. But, by nature we tend to ignore what God requires, doing what we want and failing to do his will.

- Our heavenly Father has commanded us to love him with all our heart, with all our mind, and with all our strength. But who among us has truly so loved him? Religious words slip easily from our lips, but what of the basic self-centredness of our day by day living?

When King David prayed his great prayer of confession in Psalm 32, he did not say, 'Blessed is the man who has not sinned, who has no need of forgiveness,' but rather, 'Blessed is the one whose sin is forgiven, whose debt is paid.'

Where, then, does forgiveness begin? Paul the apostle speaks of the disciples at Corinth as having been taken from a very grubby world, washed and set apart for God by the cross of our Lord. The apostle's list of the goings-on in that port city of Corinth are as ancient as they are modern. Greed, theft, drunkenness, violence, perversion and vice are all there. The church at Corinth was composed of men and women taken from such a background and yet now, wonderfully, forgiven, adopted and made members of God's holy family.

The apostle Paul uses the picture of washing as he describes how they were made clean, made acceptable before our heavenly Father. So here, in the great house, are these very practical rooms, wash rooms and bathrooms. We may need to first begin in an outside wash-house, for some of us are as well soiled as a dog that has rolled and besmirched itself in some canine delight that brings no delight to its owner and indeed makes it totally unacceptable in the house. 'A stench in the nostrils of God,' is exactly how sin, how godless ways are described in the Old Testament.

We may never have so deliberately soiled ourselves, and yet no matter how privileged, how well brought-up, how respectable we may be, when our eyes are opened, each one of us will find ourselves soiled and unacceptable before God. Isaiah, the Old Testament prophet, was both noble and godly and yet, when face to face with the glory and holiness of God, he found himself totally unacceptable, ruined and undone. The memorial stone of the godly and respected local Squire in Victorian times does not recount his many philanthropic acts of charity, but simply begins with the verse: 'God have mercy upon me a sinner.' Words that reflect his own plea before God and leave a signpost and an encouragement for those who read them today.

Why do we need forgiveness? What makes even the most privileged and refined of us totally unacceptable before God? Why are 'all our righteousnesses only as filthy rags'?

Our need of forgiveness is hard for us to see for a number of reasons. For one, if we are not guilty of specific acts like murder, theft or adultery we assume we must be fine. Then again, we are so ready and eager to forgive ourselves that we cover over or make a very small matter of any 'slight indiscretion' before God. Why, it was hardly worth noticing and we can always provide a thousand reasons why we really could not help it or why it was not our fault! The fact is that we stand accused by precisely these deep-seated, self-centred habits of mind and body to which we are, by nature, totally blind.   At rock bottom, we need forgiveness because we live in God's world as if there were no God. Perhaps not in the great crises of life or when we desperately needed something, but by and large we ignore the God in whose hand is our breath. In the words of the Lord's Prayer, we have failed to honour him, failed to seek first his kingdom and right ways, failed to do his will, much preferring to do our own will. We have also failed to love those around us in the way in which we love ourselves. These are the selfish, God-ignoring ways that the Bible calls sin, a stench, and that cause us to be totally unacceptable before him and so in desperate need of mercy and forgiveness.

The true sons and daughters of God are like street children taken from the filth, violence and vice of the city and adopted into a royal household. The first step is a complete wash and change of clothes. Here is mercy; here is the forgiveness of God, here we are given a fresh new start. Thereafter begins the very gradual, faltering process of a total change in the basis of our thinking and acting. We slowly learn to love the Lord who made us acceptable and adopted us into his family. We begin to long to please him; to put God, rather than ourselves, at the centre.

God our heavenly Father has made it wonderfully possible for us, modern disciples, to be made acceptable before him. No matter how soiled, we, too, may be made sons and daughters of the living God on the basis of mercy and forgiveness. Our Father is more willing to forgive than we are willing either to admit our need of forgiveness and humbly ask for it or to accept it when it is freely given.

'Heavenly Father, forgive us our trespasses, have mercy on us, write off our debts once and for all, put us right with yourself. May we, like the ancient Corinthian Christians, be washed and made acceptable before you.'

This is the first, great and primary application of these words. We will often need to return to confess and wash away the grime of real, everyday living in this world as a child of God, but never again for the radical treatment that first brought us into the household.

Ongoing, day by day forgiveness

As adopted members of our Father's family, we shall want to leave each day's mud behind as we enter the house. Both boot room and washroom are rooms of repentance and confession, rooms of cleansing and forgiveness. They give us a moment to reflect on the day: 'Father these are the opportunities that I missed to serve you, to honour you, to speak for you, to love my neighbour. These are the things I have failed to do. These are the things that I did in haste, anger . . . or in foolishness.' Scripture urges us not to hide or cover them over, not to belittle them as being of very minor importance, but to come openly to our heavenly Father. Such prayers are no longer in terms of our acceptability before him, our place in the family of God, but rather in terms of our walking with him at ease and in the joy of a right relationship.

If we pray it aright, the wonder of the Lord's Prayer - and, indeed, the wonder of all true Christian living - is that it will reform us, it will change us.

Sadly, there is a lot of religious activity about which does not change us at all. We go and do certain things in a compartment of our lives we call 'worship'; it may be with colour and candles and beautiful, traditional music, or it may be with stirring, modern music, shining faces and uplifted arms. We enjoy it, it moves us at the time but it does not change us, does not touch the rest of our lives. We go on living exactly as we had done before. But, for example, if we really pray the Lord's Prayer from the heart it will change us. We will find forgiveness in Christ. We will find that as we bring our trespasses day by day before God, our conscience will be awakened and sharpened. We will be more aware of our Father giving us opportunities to serve him and also of the opportunities we miss. We will begin to be aware of those things that do not bring honour to his name, even before we do them. We will begin to long not to do them. By the grace of God and the prompting of his Holy Spirit, we will be changed. This gradual changing is the purpose of God for each disciple; that we might be more Christ-like. Hence this prayer, 'Forgive us our sins, our trespasses,' will need to be often on our lips if we are to grow as disciples.

Our communal failings

Like all these petitions, the prayer for forgiveness is set in the Lord's Prayer in the plural. Although our heavenly Father chooses to deal with us one by one, we are set in communities. Like a stone thrown into a pond, we begin with personal confession, but the ripples move out to affect the whole surface. As we really begin to pray we will look beyond our own personal standing and walk before God. We will begin to see and acknowledge our collective responsibilities and failings before our heavenly Father.

For example:
-    We live in a land that has been so blessed of God. He has had such patience with us and yet, as a people, we are

turning away from him, ignoring him at every level. We cling to our materialistic lifestyle and forget the God in whose hand is our very existence . . . 'Father forgive our wilful forgetfulness of your goodness and turn us again, as a people, to godly ways.'

- We live in a land that has been the centre of an empire. We need to look afresh at our national pride and arrogance, at our deeply held community attitudes to those of other races and cultures and at our collective 'blind eye' to the commercial exploitation of those who produce the goods we buy so cheaply . . .

- We are part of a society that has become greedy and unconcerned in its use and abuse of the environment . . . 'Father forgive . . .'

- God has given the historic churches of our land very great privileges and very great spiritual responsibilities. By and large we have enjoyed the privileges and failed in our great responsibility to uphold godly ways and win the people of our land for the Lord . . . 'Father forgive the coldness, formality and absorbing self-interest of our churches and kindle afresh courage, love and vision.'

- Finally, and so significantly, we live in a society in which so many people now place the bringing up of children, and particularly their spiritual welfare, well down the list of priorities, well below the pursuit of their own career or of personal happiness. But before God the family has a far greater priority.

Our families are the basic building blocks of community living and of a godly society; the seedbed of love and stability. They are given to be the royal nursery of the rising generation. They can also be the guest rooms for godly hospitality. Our homes are the setting where godly love can be shown to our neighbour and where justice, compassion, forgiveness and faithfulness can be learned and practised by parents and children together.

In our pursuit of wealth and personal happiness, we so easily forget that our heavenly Father's priority is the raising of godly offspring. The debt we owe is to use our homes for the Lord; especially to do all in our power to faithfully bring up the youngsters he has entrusted to us to know and honour the Lord . . . 'Father, forgive us . . .'

As a land, as a church, as a society and as individuals we have fallen so far short.

'Father have mercy, forgive us our neglect, our failure, our trespasses.'

References

'To love him with all our heart' - e.g. Mark 12:28-31
Corinthians 'washed' - 1 Corinthians 6:9-11
Isaiah unacceptable before God - Isaiah 6:1-5
'God have mercy' - Luke 18:13
'Filthy rags' - Isaiah 64:6
Open confession before God - 1 John 1:5-10
Godly offspring and family priorities - Malachi 2:14-16
Bringing up youngsters - Ephesians 6:1-4

Questions

1   Where do we stand, if even the noble and godly Isaiah found himself totally unacceptable before the holiness of the Lord?

2   How natural is it to excuse, cover over or make a very small matter of our own failures before our heavenly Father?

3   'Failed to honour . . . failed to seek first his kingdom . . . failed to do his will' - to what extent is the Lord's Prayer itself a

mirror in which we can see our own need of forgiveness?

4 'A fresh new start - like street children taken, washed and adopted into the family.' How well does this describe the beginnings of discipleship?

5 What distinction is drawn between our first becoming disciples and our day by day need of forgiveness as members of the family?

6 In what ways can admitting our need of forgiveness each day enable us to grow as disciples?

7 In what particular ways is our church and our whole society in need of repentance, a turning away from wrong thinking and wrong doing, and of the forgiveness of our heavenly Father?

8 To what extent are our homes 'the royal nurseries of the rising generation'? What are our priorities in home life? Are they as God-centred as they should be?

As we forgive
... eager and ready to forgive

We have looked first at the forgiveness that God offers, as this is absolutely basic to our standing before him. We all stand before God as 'miserable sinners'; debtors in need of mercy. We come, as it were, with empty and soiled hands and with nothing to offer except the prayer, 'Forgive us our trespasses.' In his mercy, our heavenly Father clears our debts, makes us acceptable and able to stand before him. He makes us citizens of his kingdom; his adopted sons and daughters. Here is the goodness, forgiveness and mercy of God. Great and wonderful it is; more precious, says our Lord, than the finest of pearls or the greatest of treasures.

We look now at the second part, 'As we forgive those who trespass against us.' At first sight it seems as if the Lord is teaching that we can earn or deserve God's forgiveness if we forgive others. But can it mean that? Could we ever earn forgiveness before God? Before our heavenly Father even our best efforts are contaminated; our fairest offerings are only, as Isaiah so vividly describes them, 'as filthy rags'. We have fallen so far short that we are never humanly able to put things right. Reconciliation is all of God's goodness. To teach that we can earn God's forgiveness is to go against the whole teaching of our Lord and the whole of the Apostles' consistent teaching.

Rather, the Lord is reminding us that as we have known and tasted the wonderful mercy and forgiveness of God so we must reflect it in our day by day dealings with those around us. Having been forgiven we must be eager to forgive those who have wronged us. We must not be like the unmerciful servant of the Lord's story who owed his master a vastly great amount. Being totally unable to pay, he was freely and graciously forgiven, but he then went out and showed no mercy whatever to his fellow servant. The unmerciful servant was freely forgiven by his master but by his behaviour to his fellow servant he lost, he forfeited that forgiveness. We can never earn God's forgiveness. And here we are solemnly warned that our heavenly Father will not continue to have mercy on us if we ourselves remain stubbornly unforgiving.

Our Lord is teaching us to pray: 'Father, as you have forgiven me, give me a forgiving spirit.

As you have been merciful and generous to me, may I be merciful and generous to those around me.

As you have written off my debt, may I write off the debts of others. May I give them space to be real people, to make mistakes, and, by your grace, may I be willing to make the first move towards reconciliation.

May I be as ready to forgive as the father of the prodigal son who eagerly watched and waited for his son's return and rushed to forgive him.'

Such a willingness to forgive is the exact opposite of our basic human nature. We naturally demand justice, our rights, our 'pound of flesh' from others but beg for ourselves to be excused and shown mercy.

Again, the godly forgiveness we are shown here will never be easy or tidy. We will be forced on each occasion to find the right balance between the harshness of justice without mercy and the softness of mercy without justice. We are to be generous and merciful yet not to so abandon justice that people mock us or take advantage of us. Our heavenly Father well understands this, for in the cross of our Lord Jesus both justice and mercy play a full part, justice is satisfied as mercy is freely offered. We are to forgive as we have been forgiven.

In this second part of the petition we move from the wash room and boot room, where we are made acceptable, to the chapel. Here, in this quiet and lovely room, built and furnished to enable prayer to be as natural and easy as breathing, we can quietly reflect on our Father's patience and mercy towards us as we wandered and strayed or as we wilfully ignored him. Here, together or alone, we can draw strength and resolve to honour our heavenly Father in our dealings with those around us. We can resolve to be forgiving as we have been forgiven.

What does it mean 'to forgive'? The word itself means 'to send away' or 'to put away'. Forgiveness is the putting away of the things that would break us apart. The aim of forgiveness is that two persons or parties estranged by a wrong or trespass might be reconciled and brought together. To bring this about, the wrong needs to be put away. God is willing to put away our debt before him. We must be willing to put away the offences and trespasses that are committed against us; to put away, on our part, anything that would stand in the way of reconciliation.

The quiet resolve before God to be forgiving needs to be carried into the cut and thrust of daily living. And so we must move from the beauty and quietness of the chapel - where to be spiritually minded is easy - to the home, the work place and the neighbourhood where it most certainly is not.

Forgiveness of ourselves

The forgiveness of this second part of the petition is primarily about our relationship with others - and yet we do need to learn to forgive ourselves as God has forgiven us. The evil one, the accuser as he is sometimes called in scripture, will constantly play on and remind us of our past failings, our guilt, our secret sins and weaknesses or our feelings of uselessness. However true the accusations may be, once they have been brought openly before our heavenly Father and his forgiveness sought, then every time we are reminded of them and tempted to be cast down by the memory of them, our strong response must be, 'Yes, sadly true, but my heavenly Father knows about these things, the debt is paid, and all he requires is that I live today for him as his forgiven child.' If God has 'put away' our wrong doings and our failures so must we, so that we are set free to live in the present for him.

Forgiveness of those we know well

The moment we become really close to someone in friendship, courtship, marriage or as a colleague at work or leisure we discover that they are not quite perfect! It is a well established phenomenon that when a new clergyman or minister comes to a church, for the first months he is thought wonderful, fresh and bright and clearly the answer to all the church's problems, and can do nothing wrong. After a couple of years he cannot do anything right and after a couple more they know his every odd mannerism and expression so well that he is merely tolerated or ignored. You can see the wisdom of moving often! More seriously, it is a perfect illustration of the fact that when you really get to know someone you find that they are not the perfect person you imagined them to be but a frail human being with failings and weaknesses, blind spots and annoying habits. In fact, a human being in need of help and constant forgiveness.

Young people setting up home soon discover the same thing. Indeed, the first year of marriage is notoriously difficult. The lady finds that her 'prince charming,' though wonderful in the days of courtship, loses his charm as he sits sullen and unshaven over unpaid bills and cornflakes in the morning!

We need to learn forgiveness towards those closest to us. They will let us down. Our personal, treasured little ways may be upset or our possessions spoiled. We need a constant spirit of forgiveness in order to take in our stride the many annoyances. Talk them out, sort them out, but do not gather them and nurse them as growing, unforgiven resentments.

Godly leaders of a former generation referred to family life as 'the cauldron of our sanctification'; the place where true holiness of living both grows and is tested to the limit! In our homes, a willingness to ask for forgiveness, and to freely give it when it is asked of us, lies at the heart of our growth as disciples of Christ.

'Lord give me a forgiving spirit.'

Forgiveness in our society

In our neighbourhood or workplace our property may be damaged by a careless colleague, a neighbour may deliberately or unwittingly upset us, or we may be the subjects of false rumours in local gossip. The Lord is teaching us in these difficult situations to be willing to forgive; to grow, as a fruit of the Holy Spirit, a willingness to be patient; an eagerness to sort out misunderstandings in a straightforward way and to seek reconciliation.

There may be situations where reconciliation is simply not possible. We may be, or they may be 'the neighbours from hell'! To avoid spiralling and all consuming bitterness we then need either that continuing forgiveness that is the turning of a blind eye, longsuffering in New Testament language, or a willingness to change jobs or to move away and put away from our minds the whole situation.

'Lord as we have been forgiven so help us to be forgiving.'

Forgiveness of terrible wrongs

In this fallen world we can be really hurt, really let down, seriously offended against and owed much. What should we do then? What should our attitude be? In the New Testament, it comes across very clearly that there are conditions to forgiveness. The father of the prodigal son in our Lord's parable was desperately let down and yet ran to meet his son. He was ready and eager to forgive and to be reconciled with his reckless son.

However, there could be no forgiveness, no reconciliation, until that son 'came to himself' and became willing to admit his mistakes and return home. Such a willingness to face the truth and offer an apology is never easy. 'I'm sorry, I was wrong . . .' are perhaps some of the hardest words to say. It took a famine and the pigs' trough to bring the son to that point! But there must be this turning, this repentance, if there is to be any true forgiveness or reconciliation.

It is for this very reason that we pray at the beginning of a service that God would give us a genuine repentance before him. God's forgiveness is never a soft option, a papering over, but rather a reforming fire that goes to the heart of the matter and then gives us a fresh new start. Our forgiveness of those around us must reflect this.

Having said that, if those who have terribly wronged and hurt us seek our forgiveness and an opportunity to put things right, we must be as willing and as eager to forgive as the father of the prodigal son who rushed to welcome and reinstate the filthy but returning lad.

Said the apostle Peter, 'How many times shall my brother sin against me and I forgive him - seven times?' That was far more than the accepted teaching in those days. Our Lord set no limit, saying in effect, 'If your brother comes acknowledging his debt, seeking reconciliation, seeking your forgiveness, freely forgive as you have been freely forgiven.' Here is a hard lesson that does not come naturally to many of us. Indeed, in Matthew's account, after teaching the basic pattern of this prayer, the Lord immediately enlarges on this very point; the willingness of true disciples to forgive as we have been forgiven.

Moving into a yet larger scene: as God's children wanting to honour him by reflecting his mercy, what of those who deliberately hurt and maim and destroy; who deliberately steal and cheat. What of those who would scoff at your willingness to forgive and who have no intention of seeking reconciliation?

We sometimes hear people say, 'I could never forgive: . . . she cheated me of my husband . . . he cheated me of my wife . . . he abused my child . . . they killed my son. I can never, never forgive.' Think for a moment of Northern Ireland. How many heart-rending cries of anguish have been heard from that land. But supposing it was our son or our daughter, could we, should we ever forgive? Human nature cries out that those who hurt and maim and kill should never be forgiven, but how should the disciple, the forgiven child of God react?

At a Remembrance Day service in Enniskillen a bomb was detonated and a Christian man lost his lovely daughter. That father was able to bear no malice towards those who killed her. That is the Christian reaction. You cannot forgive where there is no desire for reconciliation, but you can offer it, you can be willing to forgive, you can bear no malice. Jesus himself prayed, 'Father forgive them . . .' He did not declare them forgiven. He prayed that they might come to the place where they might be forgiven, and there find forgiveness freely offered.

Agents, together, of justice and peace

'To bear no malice.' As that applies in each of our own personal lives, it also applies to groups of people. There can be great feuds between families, villages, tribes and nations; people determined never to forgive or be reconciled and living with resentment, hatred and bitterness stored up. Here is the basis of great divides, hostility and, too often, war.

What part can disciples play as God's ambassadors, God's people? Our Father's economy is always based on his people being peacemakers; praying, working and seeking for reconciliation; being willing to forgive. And so it becomes plain that forgiveness is a matter both for individual disciples and for disciples together. Hence the 'us' and 'our' and 'we' of the Lord's Prayer.

Here we move from the chapel to a favourite parlour. This is no great state room but a comfortable, informal, family room. Here, as the name suggests, members of the family talk and share and live closely with one another, sorting out family misunderstandings and chatting over common attitudes to those who for one reason or another cause us annoyance, pain or difficulty.

Although not apparently so important, the informal chat and discussion of the parlour more often than not determines what takes place, or does not take place, in the great state rooms. So, quietly, here is a most important room, its informal exchanges are the key to our relationships with one another and with the wider world.

At school my German teacher, under Hitler's regime, had lost everything - his home, parents, brothers and sisters: everything. He escaped to this country and twenty years later he was teaching German. Do you know what he was also doing? He was a godly man, and he used his position to arrange exchange groups with German families. This man had been hurt so deeply and yet here he was working for reconciliation. By the grace of God he was free from bitterness. When we have tasted the mercy of God it should begin to show in our relationships and in godly, God-honouring reactions to the great hurts of life.

This is so very difficult, flesh and blood cries out against it, but we are not taught to pray for ease. We are taught to pray day by day for godly strength to work through and overcome the deep and natural anger, resentment, bitterness and hatred and to be merciful as God, our heavenly Father, has been merciful to us. We are praying positively for a Christ-like, forgiving spirit.

Human nature finds this so hard as Dutch ex-prisoner Corrie ten Boom found, as she came face to face with a former, brutal guard of the terrible concentration camp in which she had suffered so much and in which her sister had died. She had just spoken publicly of the forgiveness of God. The former guard came forward at the end of the meeting to ask for her personal forgiveness. Corrie froze, how could he ask for such a thing! How could she ever forgive *him*! Forgiveness in such a situation is so costly, and as she was to find, only possible by the grace of God and by the power of his Holy Spirit in our lives. There is so much to come to terms with and so much to work through. Forgiveness may not be instant but it is the authentic mark of the true disciple.

This prayer for a forgiving spirit is like another great wall mirror in which we can see ourselves. It accurately reflects our relationship with our heavenly Father. It is an immediate test of our own calling and standing before God. Have we truly tasted the mercy of God? Do we long to reflect that mercy in our dealings with those around us, both in the little things and in the great hurts of life? Do we really want to see his name honoured and his kingdom come - even in the matter of forgiveness?

Although we do not know what the future holds, there was something very special in South Africa during the presidency of Nelson Mandela. Imprisoned through the dark days of apartheid for over twenty years one could reasonably expect to find a man full of hatred and bitterness; a man hungering for power to 'pay back' and 'get even with' his oppressors. To the world's wonder, on his release there emerged a man who held no malice and who in his own person embraced and brought about reconciliation, showing and calling for restraint and patience. He has acknowledged the wrongs undoubtedly done but has not looked for revenge. He has rather worked tirelessly for a new South Africa. Here is forgiveness in practice. It is personally very costly but it brings with it priceless fruit - a touch of heaven.

In the chapel we lay our lives afresh before our heavenly Father. 'May your name be honoured in my attitudes and dealings with those around me.' In the parlour we meet closely with the members of our own family, with all their imperfections, and with our sometimes dreadful fellow disciples, members of the family of God. Here in the parlour we talk over our deepest hurts and thrash out our common attitudes to those who have wronged us as a family. Humanly it would be easy to justify an attitude of contempt, hatred or revenge. But, by the grace of God, may the parlour be free from these things and marked by an openness to reason, a bearing of no malice, an eagerness for reconciliation and a willingness to forgive as we have been forgiven.

'Lord God have mercy on us. Help us to recognise our own natural and inbuilt lack of mercy. Give us a forgiving spirit. Give us grace to put away bitterness and hatred and to forgive those who trespass against us, as we have been forgiven, that your holy name may be honoured and your will done.'

As we forgive

References
'Pearls' or 'treasure' - Matthew 13:44&45
'Filthy rags' - Isaiah 64:6
The unmerciful servant - Matthew 18:23-35
Stubbornly unforgiving – Matthew 6:14&15
Conditions to forgiveness - Luke 17:3&4
The prodigal son - Luke 15:11-24
'Seven times?'- Matthew 18:21&22
Willingness to forgive - Matthew 6:14
'Father forgive them' - Luke 23:34

Questions

1   To what extent is it human nature to be like the unmerciful servant, taking forgiveness offered to us for granted but being none too hasty to forgive those around us?

2   Why should we be willing and eager to forgive?

3   How easy is it to love justice *and* show mercy?

4   Is it sometimes almost hardest of all to forgive ourselves? Yet, can we, should we, must we? Why?

5   'Not perfect, but with weaknesses, 'blind spots' and annoying habits . . . a human being in need of help and constant forgiveness.' How well does this describe those close to us? How well does it describe us?

6   'I'm sorry, I was wrong.' When these words are really meant, are they some of the hardest words to say? Why?

7   Can there be true reconciliation without a willingness to admit our mistakes?

8   'I could never, never forgive . . .' But can we 'bear no malice'? Can we be searching for and eager to welcome the first hint of a move towards reconciliation?

9   To what extent do we need to pray day by day for grace to work through and overcome our natural anger, resentment and bitterness?

10   Have you known or read about people whose Christ-like willingness to forgive has challenged you?

11   In what ways and in what situations would our heavenly Father have us be his peacemakers?

Lead us not into temptation
... surrounded by so many dangers

'Heavenly Father, lead us not into temptation.' Who or what can tempt us? What are the sources of temptation? From the prayer itself, logically, the first answer must be - God. God our heavenly Father may lead us into temptation. He will not entice us to do wrong. As the letter of James makes plain, our heavenly Father would never tempt us to do that which he hates. He may, however, lead us into situations where, because of our own passions or weaknesses, because of the enticement of those around us or because of Satan's games, we will face strong encouragement or temptation to do wrong.

Not surprisingly, many people have stumbled over these words. How can it be that God would lead us into temptation? Surely there must be some mistake? Well, in a sense, there is. It lies in our use of old and treasured words, even when they have several shades of meaning. We will be hard pressed to find a better word than the all-embracing word 'temptation', but need to bear in mind that, acknowledging our weakness, we are asking that our heavenly Father would not bring us to times of overwhelming trial or testing.

In the sense of trials and testings, temptations can be good or they can be bad. They can so easily cause us to fall. And yet, successfully resisted, they can strengthen us and enable us to grow and live more boldly for God. In this positive sense each disciple needs to grow in ability to face temptation.

For a moment we leave the splendour of the house and step outside to the coach-houses and the stable block. Great houses have always had very extensive stables, often clustered round a straw-blown stable yard. There is something particularly attractive about the scene, the warm smell of fresh straw and manure, half open stable doors, chestnut heads, the 'clomp' of a heavy horse or the light canter of a favourite pony.

It is only during this last hundred years that motor cars and tractors have replaced horses, reducing the stabling and riding of horses to a leisure pursuit. Until then almost everyone would learn to ride, as today almost everyone learns to drive. Learning to drive or learning to ride is a risky and testing time - a time of temptation.

As a son of the house learns to ride, for example, he will first be placed in the saddle of the smallest and most dependable pony and gently led a few paces. As he grows more confident the length of the halter rope can be extended, giving him greater freedom to be in charge of the pony, until the day comes when he no longer needs to be led but can be the master of his own pony. His ability to ride has been carefully matched with the trial, danger and risk of a fall. Our heavenly Father is like that, he will allow us to be tested in order to enable us to grow, to mature.

Again, there comes a time when the youngster is first allowed to ride out into the open country and onto the road. What temptation! What risk! The pony might bolt or the lad, as yet without practical experience or road sense, might gallop away in a crazy manner. Yet, unless he is allowed out of the stable yard, he will never learn to ride - and so it is with us. God is the best of fathers. His will is our ongoing growth as disciples. His aim is that we might stand strong and spiritually mature through days of temptation. We will only stand firm in such times if, before then, our heavenly Father has allowed us to grow by leading us through many times of testing and trial. Like the best of fathers God does allow us to grow, he allows us to flex our spiritual muscles. He allows us to use the spiritual sword so that we might be prepared for spiritual warfare and stand in the day of difficulty. In this sense God, our heavenly Father, leads us into temptation.

We often admire the spiritual giants among us - but it is salutary to ask them to tell of some of the many, sore trials they have faced; the trials that have brought them to the strong and radiant faith we now so envy.

As we pray, the Lord has given us an opportunity to stop and remember that we are weak and frail and set in a fallen world, a world full of danger and hurt; physical, mental and spiritual and to pray for God-given wisdom and protection. 'Lord watch over us, please keep us humbly aware of the dangers that surround us, growing in ability to face them, and safe. Do not let us be tested beyond the little we can stand.'

The double edged sword of temptation

Although temptation is always an opportunity to grow in spiritual strength and maturity, it is also a snare that would cause us to stumble. Our heavenly Father is in control of all our circumstances, poverty or plenty, war or peace, life or death. But under his hand, the world will tempt us with its delights, privileges, possessions and power. The flesh, our own anger, passions, moods, weaknesses and inner corruptions will leave us wide open to temptation. And Satan, always in the background, will seek to play on our human weaknesses and on our circumstances for his own ends.

Even a mature and able rider can be thrown by a slip, a stone, a branch or a frightened horse. The most mature disciple is equally vulnerable. We do need to learn to walk humbly; to pray frequently for protection, discernment, wisdom and grace. In this petition our Lord teaches us to do so.

Behind our daily, small temptations to stray from God's holy ways lies the great temptation to rebel against God. We may be gently lured away little by little, like sheep eating one desirable patch of grass after the next, until we have strayed far from godly ways and thinking. Alternatively we may come under great pressure to deny the faith and turn our back on God. In the Old Testament, the great temptation of Job to 'curse God and die' was of this nature. Pray that our heavenly Father would spare us from such terrible temptation. Pray for those imprisoned even now for their faith and enticed with the promise of 'instant freedom' if they will deny their faith and assent to some other faith, philosophy or world view. The great tribulation of which the New Testament warns must be of this nature; times when Satan and his servants do all in their power to seduce, crush and disinherit the saints of God.

Temptation from the world

The world around us is our great testing ground, for it cares nothing for God or godly ways. It will present us with an attractive and brightly-lit, supermarket display of alternative lifestyles, faiths and world views. Like shoppers we are enticed and urged to choose for ourselves and be uncritical of the choices of others. True Christianity, judged to have passed its sell-by date, is generally no longer stocked. But the world will present us with a 'museum corner' of musty and outdated hymn books, damp and dark churches, strange robes and rituals that have little or no bearing on real life.

The world will also tempt us with short cuts to fame and fortune; offer to make each of us instant millionaires and owners of our own stately home. It will tempt us with sharp practice in business and less than integrity in dealing with other people's money. Although the law and codes of practice aim to restrict gross malpractice there will always be the pressure and the powerful temptation to search for loopholes or weak points in the fence of the law or places where it can be 'moved a little' for our personal or corporate gain. In business and at home we will be tempted to put ourselves first and regard everyone else as 'disposable'. Trust and honourable dealing are closely tied to godliness and so for the disciple, the Christian, this fallen world presents a whole minefield of temptation.

Temptation from within

Our own flesh will tempt us in so many ways. We will be enticed to throw off the 'inhibitions of godliness' and seek 'self-fulfilment', self-gratification at every level. We will be tempted to be carried along by our moods and feelings. Anger, resentment and 'black moods' take a conscious effort to manage in a God-honouring way, but the temptation will always be to give them free rein, to give vent to our feelings by 'taking it out' on those around us.

We will be enticed to throw off 'outdated morality', enjoy ourselves and be 'free'. Being human we will be sorely tempted to cut free from the narrow path of discipleship and join in. 'And do I not burn with passion,' says the apostle Paul as he speaks of another man's fall.

King David, a full-blooded warrior, sent his troops to fight while he spent an idle spring in Jerusalem. Looking out from the roof-top resting place of his royal house his eyes fell on a beautiful woman bathing - maybe she intended it to be that way. The temptation was overwhelming . . . and the outcome: adultery, intrigue, manslaughter and a home-life dogged with difficulty.

In the course of his duty, Joseph, as a young and attractive slave in Egypt, found himself passionately desired by his master's wife. (The occupational hazard of a resident helper or 'au pair'. . . !) For Joseph the invitations were incessant, the opportunities plentiful but, by the grace of God, he stood his ground holding his master's marriage in honour: 'Far be it from me to sin against heaven and my master.' The lady's determination and passion grew and the moment came when Joseph's priority was to get out, to escape. Says scripture, 'Flee fornication,' unashamedly run from it. Faced with the devil, stand your ground, but faced with immorality show your heels. Sometimes we need to get out, whatever the taunts or threats. For Joseph it meant prison, but under the hand of God it was also the pathway by which he was lead to great usefulness. God honours those who honour him.

Spiritual warfare

The world will squeeze us into its mould, the flesh is weak and vulnerable and Satan, who plays on our circumstances, whatever they are, will turn them to trip us.

We deceive ourselves so easily and are blissfully unaware of the dangers in which we stand. Like little children who will just run into a road, we so easily run into a situation in which we are overwhelmed by difficulty or temptation. That is exactly what happened to the apostle Peter. Jesus had warned him that Satan would tempt him, but said Peter; 'Lord, they may fall away, but I will stand firm even to death.' Peter did not know himself, or the overwhelming nature of temptation. He did not know the danger into which he was running. He was so sure of his own strength that he rushed into terrible testing. Then, confronted by ordinary people who identified him as one of Jesus' disciples, the great apostle totally collapsed.

However, before you condemn Peter, put yourself in his position. The Lord had been violently arrested and was facing death. The accusation is made: 'You were there. You are one of them.' How would you react? It is easy to point the finger at Peter but, if on your immediate answer, hung imprisonment or freedom, life or death, would it not appear 'wiser' to say, 'I never knew him.' The temptation is absolutely overwhelming and that is the nature of temptation. Yet, like Peter, we so easily rush into it. They were no fools who taught us to pray morning by morning, '. . . that we might fall into no sin neither run into any kind of danger.'

- If we are young we will be invited many times to join the party: 'Enjoy yourself. Break free. Forget God and the narrow path of faith'

- If we are poor we may be sorely tempted to steal or deceive to obtain what we feel we need: 'They have so much more than I do, I have a right to take it . . .'

- If we are fit and well we will be tempted to forget God in the whirl of sport, family, pleasure or business life.

- If we are successful and rich, we will be tempted to put God out of our thinking: 'I have no longer any need of God.'

- Should we fall seriously ill, we will be tempted to self-pity, to murmur against those who are looking after us: 'They do not really care. They have not noticed how terrible I feel this morning or that I need . . .' Self pity is the temptation matched exactly to those who are unwell. The same temptation may be directed towards God - to doubt his goodness: 'If God really cared, would he leave me in this situation?' - or to doubt his power: 'God does not seem able to help me.'

- Finally, when we are in our last days, we may be tempted to be grasping and possessive, hanging on to old ways, things and the people we still have: 'How could you think of going out and leaving me all alone for two whole hours?'

There is an almost infinite variety of temptations each presented by, and hence precisely matched to, our particular situation. It is for this reason that other people's temptations are always so much easier to face than our own! Their temptations would never trip us up but our own are much more difficult. Each temptation, each time of testing, is an opportunity to grow, to make a God-honouring response . . . or to tumble.

Our Lord is teaching us that we need to be aware, as Peter was so blissfully unaware, that we are frail and vulnerable and open to attack. He is teaching us to recognise that the world, the flesh and Satan will test us sorely, teaching us to take each situation to our heavenly Father before we set out. Jesus is teaching us to pray, as he prayed in the garden before his arrest. He prayed but Peter did not. He is teaching us to pray for courage, guidance and protection and teaching us to pray that our heavenly Father's will may be done as we face each new and testing situation.

Praying for one another

Again, do notice that we are not just praying for ourselves. Here, as throughout the Lord's Prayer, it is 'us' and 'our' not 'me' and 'my'. Certainly, 'Lead me not into temptation,' as I meet with such and such a situation or person, but also 'us' and 'our'. Kingdoms, countries, multinational companies and churches are all being constantly tested and can all be sorely tempted. In the far reaching decisions that are made in parliaments, boardrooms and committees the temptations for short-term gain, for exploitation, for worldly but ungodly ways are very great. The church itself is constantly tempted to be a mere religious mirror of the secular society in which it lives, to follow the latest moral or political fashion or to be less than straightforward in its handling of money. Therefore pray that they, or we, as we play our part, may not be led into temptation, but may stand with godly integrity and courage. Such prayers have by no means passed their sell-by date!

Finally, in the opening chapter of the Old Testament book of Job, we are shown Job praying for his family. He is praying for his sons in their eating and drinking and making merry. 'Lord God, there are so many dangers, lead them not into temptation, forgive them where they have fallen, keep them safe.' What a helpful pattern for our own praying.

The Lord himself, in the garden before his arrest urged the disciples to pray that they might not fall into temptation. He also prayed for them. 'Peter, Satan has desired to sift you as wheat is sifted, to test and tempt you very severely, but I have prayed for you'.

'But I have prayed for you.' How many of us have cause to thank God for those who prayed for us in worldly, fleshly, God-forgetting days as Satan sought to test us. I thank God for a praying grandmother who prayed while I wandered blissfully unaware through the spiritual minefield of student days.

'Father, we pray that you would keep us, and those we care about, safe. May we not be squeezed by the world, ruled by the flesh or manipulated by Satan to do what seems expedient or desirable in the moment, but live and act by godly principle. Give us increasing discernment, wisdom and courage to live for you day by day.'

References
God tempts no one - James 1:13
'Curse God' - Job 1:11, 2:5 & 2:9
The great tribulation - Matthew 24:21 & Revelation 7 13-17
'And do I not burn'
        (with passion or indignation) - 2 Corinthians 11:29
David tempted - 2 Samuel 11:2-5
Joseph tempted - Genesis 39:6-20
'Flee fornication' - 1 Corinthians 6:18
Those who honour him - 1 Samuel 2:30
Jesus warning Peter - Luke 22:31-34
Peter's temptation - Luke 22:55-62
Job and his family - Job 1:4&5
'To sift you as wheat' - Luke 22:31

Questions
1 In what ways and to what purpose can our heavenly Father lead us into, and through, times and situations of sore temptation?

2 For the disciple of Christ, in what sense is the whole of life temptation?

3 How can this petition humble us and so help us to cope with our natural spiritual pride?

4 Which particular temptations does our own society forcefully present to us?

5 Does the desire 'to be ourselves', 'to freely express and be the person our genes and environment would make us', need to be brought under the control of our Lord's call to holiness of living, taking up our cross daily and following him?

6 Joseph, chased by his master's wife, had to make some hard choices. For what two reasons did he refuse to do as she asked? Can these reasons be useful to us? Could Joseph's situation serve as a useful warning to us about living in another person's

house? . . . or even what could happen when someone comes to live in ours?

7   Does God still honour those who honour him?

8   Strong and blustering Peter rushed into terrible temptation - would we have done any better had we been in his situation?

9 Why are other people's temptations no great problem to us when our own are so difficult?

10   In what ways does it help us if we recognise that, despite our apparent self-reliance and strength, we are actually frail and vulnerable and open to attack?

11   What value is there in praying for our friends, our families and for one another that we do not fall into temptation?

Keep us, deliver us from evil
... safety in an evil world

We live in a world that is at the same time glorious and tragic. It is a wonderful world with so much that is noble, pure and breathtakingly beautiful; but it is also a fallen world, a world shot through with suffering and injustice, malice and evil. God our heavenly Father understands the evil we face as does our Lord who taught us to pray these words.

The Lord of Glory humbled himself and came among us. He shared our life, experienced the pain of rejection, hatred and grave injustice; he faced the most excruciating death in order to free us from the grip and power of evil.

Hell is the ultimate evil and our heavenly Father knows, as we do not, its depth and its horror. He gave his only Son to rescue us from that ultimate evil. God our heavenly Father is the great deliverer, our Saviour.

Despite their loveliness great houses have always been vulnerable to all kinds of troubles. They are vulnerable to troubles from within, from members of the family itself or from those employed in the running of the house, among whom may be those who would deceive, steal or even destroy the household. They are also open to troubles from without, from people who would break in and help themselves to treasures, antiques or important papers and from those who would break in to hurt or destroy.

In the kingdom of heaven, as with a great house, our happiness and our security lies in knowing the dangers we face and in being watchful and on our guard. So, from the warmth and wonder of our heavenly Father's goodness to us and purposes for us, we must turn to be forewarned of the evil depths of our own hearts, of the sheer hatred of evil people and of the malice and cunning of Satan.

The prayer, 'Deliver us from evil,' is consistently found in the texts of the gospel of Matthew and expands the previous petition. We have prayed that we might not be led into overwhelmingly evil situations, now we pray for protection and for deliverance within them.

Firstly, our Lord taught us to plead for rescue from the thoughts, words and deeds that are conceived, spoken and done almost before we realise what is happening.

i) 'Deliver us from evil thinking.'

It was the great German reformer Martin Luther who taught us that we cannot stop the birds flying over our heads, but we can stop them nesting in our hair!

It is the nature of these brilliant things we call our brains to be constantly turning over all kinds of ideas, often quite unconsciously. All sorts of ideas 'just arrive' but it is our responsibility before our heavenly Father to either develop them or expel them. Brilliant ideas and useless ideas; wonderful, godly and selfless ideas or vile, evil and destructive ideas are constantly entering our conscious minds either to be enjoyed, delighted in and turned into action; or to be rejected and thrown out.

These ideas are inspired by all that we see, hear and feel. They are inspired by our present situation or by the lovely or terrible experiences of the past; inspired by our heavenly Father or thrown in like a hand grenade by the evil one to wreak destruction. However they come to arrive, the kind of ideas presented by our sub-conscious minds will be influenced by what we feed into them and by what we welcome from them.

The kind of birds overhead depend on where we choose to walk. Walk in the country in the early morning and you may well be greeted by the skylark, walk in the city square and mind the pigeons, walk by the coast and watch the gulls wheel and swoop over your head. In the same way the kind of ideas that flood into our minds depend on where we put ourselves. They are influenced by the kind of people we mix with, the magazines and papers we read, the films and programmes we watch. All these will influence the ideas that flood into our minds. If you throw bread in the city, you are inviting the pigeons to settle. If you throw bread at the coast, the gulls will be around you in less than a moment.

We may actively choose to restrict our conscious thinking to all that is good, honourable and worthy of praise, as the apostle Paul urges us to. Alternatively, we may invite other 'birds' to settle. We may welcome and revel in very negative and destructive thoughts about ourselves or about the motives and intentions of those around us. Allowing thoughts like these to grow and develop lies at the root of so many of the difficulties in our relationships with one another.

By our choice of cinema, television, video and computer viewing our sub-conscious minds are flooded with very powerful images for good . . . or for evil. We live in days when we watch and regard as 'entertainment' violence, vice and evil, but are amazed and horrified when people put the very fantasies we enjoy into practice in the real world.

At this more dramatic level, we may 'so throw our bread' as to encourage our sub-conscious minds to supply us with unrestrained fantasies of financial or political power, of sex or of violent revenge. They will respond accordingly, supplying ideas to achieve our chosen end, be it superglue in a neighbour's lock or guns in school.

The potential is within each of us, for out of the heart comes all that is pure, noble and lovely but out of the heart comes also every evil thought: unkindness, uncleanness, theft, envy and murder. All these come from within. Both Judas' betrayal of his Lord and Hitler's 'final solution', the extermination of the Jewish people, were once 'just a thought.'

'Lord deliver us from evil thinking, rescue us from

feeding and revelling in that which is evil. Wake us up so that we may recognise the poison of evil thinking for what it is. Give us strength, despite its fascination, to turn it off, kick it out, to scare away such 'birds', before they 'nest' and become destructive words or deeds, wreaking havoc in our homes, our lives or our society . . . Father, keep us from evil.'

ii) 'Deliver us from evil speaking.'

A retired missionary was telling how the Lord first challenged him. As a lad of sixteen, he was with his friends on a train. They were 'proving their manhood' by loudly outdoing one another in foul language. A man in the corner was totally ignored but, as he left the carriage, he very quietly said to the future missionary, 'Young man, if your heart is as evil as your mouth, you are in very great trouble.'

From our lips escape too easily all kinds of evil: words that are lying or deceitful; words that crush and destroy; words that are foul or words that throw into the gutter something that is holy or to be cherished.

Too many relationships are destroyed by an unrecognised habit of evil speaking! We are commanded to love and build one another up and yet self-centred, arrogant, critical and destructive words so easily escape our lips: 'What is the matter with you!' 'You've done it again!' 'You're useless!' or in their absence, 'He'll never be any good!' 'He's rubbish!'

'Lord set a watch on our lips, keep us from evil speaking, to one another and of one another.'

iii) 'Deliver us from evil deeds.'

Evil deeds may be done for all kinds of hidden reasons. We may be blinded to what we are doing by sickness, by the heat of lust or of anger or by an all consuming commitment to a cause. In lust and in anger we only think of ourselves. In the total devotion to a political, racial or religious cause it is all too easy to lay aside the godly principles of kindness, courtesy, justice and mercy. We assume that belonging to our group gives us the right to treat other groups of people unkindly, discourteously or with contempt. We do to them what we would not like done to ourselves.

The Lord warned his disciples that they would be persecuted and even put to death by men who were really convinced that they were doing it 'for God'. St. Paul was such a man when, as Saul the zealous Pharisee, he persecuted the Christian believers. Many a man, like Saul, has done terrible evil, believing it to be right, because he has done it for a political or religious 'cause'.

Harshness, hatred and persecution, beatings, burnings, imprisonments and shootings. . . 'Father, keep us from evil.'

Biologically, we are sexual beings. For some this provides no challenge at all to godly living. Others, however, find themselves from time to time driven by all but overpowering sexual urges and desires. In this fallen world we may have a very heavy cross to carry. Here is a prayer that, by the grace of God, we may so manage ourselves that we are kept from evil deeds.

In the partnership of godly marriage our heavenly Father has provided the right setting to find human fulfilment at every level. In essence Christian marriage is the commitment of a man and a woman before God, witnessed by those who know them best, that they will faithfully and exclusively share the whole of life together until death.

It seems that social custom and current legislation are increasingly keeping otherwise committed couples from godly marriage. Do we need to free couples who are seeking the commitment of marriage from the great display and expense that society currently demands of 'a wedding'? Again, do we we need to do all we can to strongly encourage the government, by its financial legislation, to underpin godly marriage rather than undermine it.

Sexual drive is like a fire. In the hearth or boiler of our home it can give warmth and comfort, whilst outside of godly marriage, it can burn like a fire out of control, raging and driving all before it. Unchecked and unmanaged, our sexual urge and lust can drive us to all kinds of evil. It can lead to all sorts of ungodly partnerships; to unfaithfulness within marriage and to the breaking of other homes and marriages by adultery. In the extreme it can lead to perversion or child abuse. Here is a prayer that we may face our sexual nature and so channel it that it burns only in the God-given hearth of the marriage partnership and does not become a force for evil, destroying our own and other people's lives.

'Father, whatever lies behind, help us from now on to channel and manage our strong passions and desires in ways that please you. Keep us from evil.'

Closely linked is that other wild horse, anger. Anger is the characteristic of the young man which, wild and untamed, leads to so much hurt and destruction. However, 'broken-in' and under control it can enable us to stand with strong and godly passion against oppression and evil. It was in godly anger that the Lord cleared the temple of thieving money changers and crooked salesmen who had made the house of prayer a den of thieves. It was with godly passion that William Wilberforce and his colleagues fought for the abolition of slavery. It is this kind of godly anger that has driven all the great social reformers.

Many of us are social creatures and strongly need to belong to an organisation, group or gang. However, it is too easy to link with a group where the pressure from our peers is to do wrong, to do evil. In youth it is so easy to be swept into heavy drinking, the misuse of drugs, theft or violence.

Scripture strongly warns us to avoid being caught up in a crowd and swept into doing evil.

To provide for our social need, our heavenly Father has given us a 'gang' or family. It is the fellowship of his church and in it, despite its many imperfections, we are called to care about one another, to forgive one another and to encourage one another to work as a team for his kingdom.

Holiness of living and true discipleship are all about bringing our natural and biological inclinations, desires and lusts under the lordship of Christ. It is a matter of putting to death or denying ourselves all that our Father hates, or, as our Lord so memorably put it, of taking up our cross daily and following him.

'Lord God give us grace and patience to bring our driving passions under your control. Keep us from evil thinking, evil speaking and evil deeds.'

Secondly, our Lord taught us to plead for rescue from evil from without. To pray for rescue from evil people, evil days and from the evil one.

i) 'Lord, deliver us from evil men and women.'

The driving force behind the desire for leadership is the desire for power; power over people, power to influence and change lives, power to rule and direct. Like so many things, such power is two edged, it can be channelled and used for great good or it can be used for great evil. Here is a prayer that our heavenly Father would keep us from using the authority entrusted to us in our homes, at our work or in the wider society for evil. It is also a prayer that he would keep us safe from those who are using their position of power for evil.

The evil abuse of power can be as close at hand as a stronger brother or sister, a parent, step-parent or someone in a parent's place. It can be a bully, a teacher, a lecturer or someone at work. It can be the leaders of a gang or organisation. It can be evil people in senior management, or indeed in government.

Evil at home turns the place of love and safety into a prison house of fear, violence and abuse. At work, an evil 'boss', shop steward or group turns a place of creativity into a place of stress and abuse at every level.

In the church evil men, 'wolves' as both our Lord and the apostle Paul call them, may be charming, eloquent and persuasive as they gain power over us, 'relieve' us of our money or lead us astray theologically or morally.

In society, where at best we support and encourage one another, how unthinkably terrible it is to come under the power of terrorists or to be under a death threat from evil religious extremists, caught up by a violent gang, or hemmed in by an organised crime ring. We do well to thank God daily if we know nothing of such things and to pray that he would keep us safe. We need to cry to God daily if we find ourselves, or know of fellow disciples, trapped by such evil, at home, at work or in the wider society.

Sometimes, 'Deliver us from evil' will be a cry for godly wisdom, strength and protection within a terrible situation. Sometimes it will be a prayer for courage and a godly way of escape, for the New Testament unashamedly urges us to escape from evil oppression. Sometimes it will be a prayer for those we know who are caught up in evil.

Sometimes this petition will be a cry from the heart as far-reaching, perhaps national, choices, decisions and appointments are made. 'Lord, spare us from evil leaders and from evil laws.' For nationally, too, we do well to pray that our heavenly Father would keep us from evil. How terrible it was for godly men and women to be caught up under Hitler and the Nazi regime on the far right of politics, or under Stalin and the Communists on the far left. How almost impossibly hard it is for a Christian, especially for a Christian leader, to live for the Lord under an evil regime be it atheistic or religious. 'Lord, deliver us . . .'

'Father deliver us . . .' can also be a cry, from within an evil situation, to deliver us from the natural anger and resentment that wells up in our own hearts towards those who threaten and abuse us - in itself an evil that would destroy us. From the prison camps have come many accounts of those who, by the grace of God, have learned to rise above the malice and hatred of the camp and be free before God to pray for, and even to love, those who taunted and persecuted them.

The Lord's Prayer is not about sweet sentiment. It is about the glorious and terrible reality of living for our heavenly Father in this fallen and often evil world. It is an essential prayer for safety and deliverance for ourselves, our families, our land and our fellow disciples throughout the world.

'Lord deliver us from evil men and women in positions of power, and from our own ungodly response to the evil we experience in our day by day living.'

ii) *'Lord, deliver us from, and in, the evil day.'*

The evil day is the day of personal or social calamity. 'Lord, spare us that we may live free and unfettered lives for you' - for the day of calamity narrows our vision so that we strive only for our own survival.

The evil day is the day we hear from the doctor that our remaining days are very short. It is the day of domestic calamity; the day we learn the terrible truth of trust betrayed, or witness the sudden death of those we had loved with all our heart. Although we must all walk through the valley of the shadow of death, it is the promise of our heavenly Father to walk with us. We need fear no evil. Nevertheless we are taught to pray that our Father would spare us from such overwhelming evil.

Evil days can touch a whole nation; days of financial ruin, days of famine or days of war with the accompanying loss of home, loss of loved ones, loss of everything. The whole book of Job wrestles with such evil days; days of utter calamity.

'Father we thank you for every day that you spare us from these things. Things that, in this fallen world may touch our lives at any time. Help us to use the good days you give us for the honour of your name and walk closely with us through the dark days. By your grace, bring us safely through them.'

References

'Good, honourable' etc. - Philippians 4:8
'Theft, murder, envy' etc. - Mark 7:21-23
Murder, 'for God' - John 16:1-3
Saul persecuting Christian believers
           - Acts 8:1-3 & 1 Timothy 1:12-15
Clearing the temple - Luke 19:45&46
In a crowd bent on evil - Exodus 23:2
'Wolves' - Matthew 7:15, Acts 20:29, 2 Peter 2:1-3
Escape evil oppression - Mark 13:14
With us in the valley of the shadow - Psalm 23

Questions
Our thoughts
1 Would it be good if all the thoughts that pass through our minds were known to those around us?

2 What kind of negative and destructive thoughts, allowed to grow and develop, might destroy ourselves, our home lives or our working relationships?

3 How do we feed our minds? How do we regard the fantasy world of the magazine, television or computer?

4 How can we control what we think about?

Our words
5 How evil are our mouths? Do we cheapen godly or precious things by the way in which we speak?

6 Do we use our words to encourage and build up or to crush and destroy?

Our deeds
7 Saul persecuted the early Christian believers out of religious zeal. Are there people that we despise or treat unfairly? How can we keep ourselves from such evil?

8 Can our strong sexual passions lead us to do evil?

9 What has our heavenly Father provided to be the right place for passionate love and to keep us from such evil?

10 What good and what evil can come from anger? Can you name some examples?

Other people
11 How deep in human nature is the desire for power?

12 Can you think of examples in which people have used their power, a) for great good, b) for great evil?

13 How much are we aware or concerned about our fellow disciples who are being evilly oppressed?

14 How natural is it to return evil for evil, hatred for hatred? How can we begin to cope?

Evil days
15 Why and how does the evil day narrow our vision?

Keep us from evil, *continued*
... the one who would destroy

A heart that readily wells up with evil dreams and plans, flesh that delights in them, a fallen world that brings to us all kinds of evil days, people, circumstances and opportunities . . . and in the shadows, hiding behind all these things is Satan, the evil one. In scripture he is also described as the deceiver and the destroyer. In the Lord's Prayer it is legitimate to translate, 'deliver us from evil,' 'deliver us from the evil one.' We wrestle not only with flesh and blood but with mighty, deceptive and destructive spiritual forces under the evil one.

Satan and temptation

Satan is the master of his art. His constant aim is to cause us to stumble. Behind Job's terrible trials was Satan seeking to cause Job to curse God to his face. Behind Peter's terrible night, as he found himself denying his Lord, was Satan seeking to cause Peter to fall. Yet on the surface, all could be accounted for by personal weaknesses, by the pressure and persuasion of the people around them or by the circumstances in which they found themselves.

All sorts of people will be employed in a great house, each of them carefully selected for their particular role. Yet, occasionally, beneath the courteous exterior may lie great danger; a servant or servants with a hidden agenda, servants whose secret loyalties lie elsewhere and whose actual aim is to destroy the household. And so it is with the kingdom of God.

We are guests in our heavenly Father's world and yet Satan, a fallen servant of God, will constantly tempt us, both individually and together as groups, races and nations, to grasp, take and recklessly exploit this word for ourselves. Again, God has commanded us to care for one another, yet we will be constantly tempted to use and exploit one another.

How would you handle it if, when staying as a guest in a great house, you were to be approached by a servant who privately invites you to his office. With great skill and charm he shows you an apparently genuine document that indicates that, if you follow his instructions, the whole property could become yours. He suggests that your rights are being denied you. Just as you have been invited to share openly in the life of the family, now, by treachery, you are invited to claim for yourself whatever you will. You turn your back and try to forget it, but the idea will not go away. You have new eyes. All that was previously offered to be innocently appreciated and enjoyed, could now be yours for the taking.

This is exactly the picture given to us in the third chapter of Genesis. Satan suggests that God's commands are irksome and restricting; that God is denying a basic 'right', namely, to do as we will, to be as gods. Satan now offers this 'right' for the taking. He tempts us to break free from God and do as we will. Here is Satan's basic ploy. See how he uses it again and again.

Satan and society

In modern Western culture, with our great Christian heritage, perhaps the most effective way in which the evil one has been at work is by way of ungodly liberal thinking. Here is a way of thinking that cuts free from God and his fatherly commands and instructions. By it Satan has been able to bring our godly heritage all but tumbling down.

Liberal thinking has laid aside absolute, godly moral values, such as the Ten Commandments, and replaced them with a whole sea of relative values. These are human values that simply depend on current social thinking, the circumstances in which we find ourselves, or on the whim of a ruling party or dictator. Such thinking is always presented very plausibly and forcefully and yet it has exposed us to a flood of evil right across society.

In Britain, ungodly liberal thinking underlies the throwing off of godly ways and a sliding back into old and pagan ways right across the moral spectrum. Godly chastity before marriage and faithfulness within it are being displaced by a widespread thinking which regards the exclusive and lifelong commitment of marriage as of little importance, stable partnerships being the normal pattern. It is a way of thinking that can lead to the collapse of godly family life, and unltimately to the collapse of society.

How far will we slide? Roman society women dated the year by the name of the then current partner. Indeed, the ancient Romans accepted any partner, homosexual or heterosexual, at any time with children, of mixed parentage, loosely attached along the way. For our encouragement, this was the very seedbed or cradle of the New Testament church.

In Roman times, Christian disciples were a people with a new and distinctive way of living. However, the effect in our own days of declining godliness is, *firstly*, to make appear 'very odd' those Christian disciples 'still living' our heavenly Father's narrow but best way and, *secondly*, to alienate great swathes of people, who have nothing against the church, but find themselves excluded from it by the way in which they choose to live.

There is a very great social cost attached to the prevailing godless way of thinking. It has undermined the family, offering 'equally valid' alternative lifestyles, but they are lifestyles that tend to the breaking down of society. These liberal lifestyles have produced, often not of their own choosing, many more single parents and homeless teenagers. This flows from the casual nature of modern parenting partnerships where one or the other may move on or be replaced, and youngsters find that the new relationship in some way excludes them. This casual or uncommitted approach has also given us a spiralling tax burden that the rest of society must pay to care for those who are no longer in economically efficient, mutually supporting families.

This tide of secular thinking has also destroyed so much that was orderly, good and godly in the education of our young people, particularly at the primary level. It has added to godly honest dealing a range of 'creative' financial approaches. It has brought into medicine what is in practice abortion on demand, the 'right' to destroy a dependent life that is not wanted, a way of thinking naturally to be extended to euthanasia. It has filled our society with groups demanding rights of every kind, and has largely taken away the sense of personal responsibility or duty. In short, ungodly liberal thinking has brought with it a whole rising tide of evil. And behind it, Satan smiles as he sees the godly values in our society being steadily undermined.

'Father, spare us, rescue us from evil. Turn us again as a nation to hunger after that which is godly and to leave behind that which is evil. Raise up godly men and women who will stand against the tide of evil. Help us to pray as you would have us pray, not to pray and wring our hands in impotent lament, but to pray and then, with courage, play our part. May your name be honoured, your kingdom come, your will be done.'

For many years our heavenly Father has protected this country from evil, surrounded it and kept it safe, but how can we expect the continued blessing of God in this privileged way and yet turn our back on him? Disciples of Christ need earnestly to pray, 'Keep us from evil. Deliver us from the evil ways and evil influences to which we as a nation, in our God-forgetting and all-tolerant way, have laid ourselves wide open.'

Satan and the church

Within the church the strategies of the evil one have been very effective. By the same ungodly liberal thinking, he has undermined true faith in great sections of the church, offering well-presented human teaching which displaces the teaching of our Lord and his apostles. By this thinking, for example, he has torn apart the church over the central issues of Christian belief, over the ministry of women and the acceptability of homosexual practice.

In our worship, Satan, the deceiver, delights to replace sincerity of heart and holiness of life with splendour of ceremony or with heat of emotion.

In our fellowships, at every opportunity, Satan, the destroyer, sows those fast-growing weeds of mistrust, discord and envy. How we need to be constantly on our guard, praying that 'we may agree in the truth of God's holy word and live in unity and godly love'; testing all we hear and read against the plain teaching of scripture, and actively guarding our fellowship with one another. Satan delights both to lead us astray and to divide us. He delights to see the church, at the local level and at the national level, destroying itself.

Satan and ourselves

In our individual lives, the evil one plays on our anxieties, fears and hardness of heart in order to undermine or destroy our walk with our heavenly Father and our walk with our fellow disciples. This world really is a spiritual mine-field!

Satan works indirectly through material wealth, pleasure, anxiety or the pressures of life, to make us forgetful, fruitless and cold towards the things of God. It is for these reasons that it is so hard for the successful person, modern and materialistic, to enter the kingdom of heaven. It is for these reasons that young Christian disciples, who begin so full of vision and passion for God, end up in middle-life cold, indifferent and fruitless. 'Father, keep us from evil.'

Satan works more directly as the destroyer as he presents ideas and convictions that would wreck our walk with our heavenly Father or our usefulness in his service. The recorded temptations of our Lord are exactly of this pattern. Each, though presented as apparently highly desirable, would have either destroyed him or his work. He was tempted to use his authority and power to gratify his personal need, at that moment his hunger. He was tempted to commit a spectacular suicide and so destroy himself. And finally he was tempted, in the privacy of the moment, to gain all he desired at the price of becoming a double agent, a secret servant of Satan.

We will face similar times of testing. For us, the temptations of Satan can be presented as the persuasive argument of an atheist, the advice of a 'friend', or simply a 'gut feeling'. The 'sudden resignation syndrome' is a typical response to satanic attack. A faithful disciple doing a useful work and keen to walk closely with their heavenly Father, is suddenly convinced that it is God's will that they should give up - and they do so, without warning and without handing over to others. The work is weakened if not destroyed and Satan, the destroyer and great deceiver, has scored a hit. Beware of sudden overwhelming convictions of this kind! Our heavenly Father is a God of order not of chaos. We can walk with him in quietness and in confidence.

More rarely, but dramatically, Satan works as the destroyer through tricks of the mind. He is sometimes behind quite overwhelming and terrifying thoughts of destruction, both of ourselves and of those around us. Fiery darts indeed, to be recognised by their sudden force and destructiveness. Our heavenly Father does not shout at us! So if, when you are under great stress, depressed or just very tired, you feel a strong prompting to 'Finish it all, throw yourself in front of this train,' - hold fast. If it is, 'I could kill you,' - hold fast. If it is, 'Drive into the ditch, now,' - keep steady. Or, in the early hours you might wake from a dream with a mind filled with the most unthinkable scenes of violence or vice, from which you recoil in horror. Such things are by no means uncommon, but they are not of God. 'Lord, deliver us from evil. Keep us safe, keep us steady.'

Even more directly, if we have in some way played into Satan's hands, we may find ourselves or come across others who are directly under the influence, even control of the evil one. We can so easily bite on his bait for it is always presented so attractively. As a former generation put it, 'Satan's delicacies are always served on silver salvers.' It is so desirable to know the future; to have hidden powers; to be in touch with the spirits; to be in contact with those we have lost through death. Yet to pursue any of these is to bite on Satan's bait.

We are involved in spiritual warfare where powerful spiritual agencies would enthrall us, ensnare us and enlist us for their own ends and purposes. They may offer us 'the world', as Satan offered our Lord. They may offer all we could desire as Satan offered in the garden, but the aim is always to lure us from single hearted loyalty to our heavenly Father. Is this a warning to us of the possible, hidden danger behind an invitation to join a secret brotherhood or lodge, or even behind certain job or financial offers?

Said the Lord to Peter, 'Pray that you do not fall into temptation.' Peter slept well - and fell. It is not for nothing that our Lord taught us to pray, 'Lead us not into temptation but deliver us from evil.'

The early chapters of Genesis tell us that, after their fall, both the man and the woman hid themselves. After such an encounter with Satan's temptation, whether we fall or not, it takes very great courage to come to our heavenly Father in honest and open confession. It takes great courage to lay before him all the circumstances that led up to such a sore temptation and all the subsequent thoughts of our hearts and deeds of our bodies. To make such a confession is the very last thing we would choose to do. To hide, belittle or cover it all over seems a much more attractive proposition. And yet our Father does not look on the outward appearance of respectability but on the heart. In the kingdom of heaven there are no hidden secrets and there are no double agents.

If we have been caught by the evil one we need to cry to our heavenly Father for mercy. Deliverance and forgiveness are freely available, they have been purchased for us by the cross of the Lord Jesus. To be given them demands very courageous openness with our heavenly Father, from whom nothing is hidden. It takes great courage, but, for those who dare, for those who come to him hiding nothing, he has promised forgiveness and a fresh new start. The wonderful truth is that there are no depths of evil, into which we may have fallen, from which the grace of God cannot rescue us.

Keep us from the evil one

'Father, have mercy on us, deliver us, rescue us. Keep us safe from evil, evil from within and evil from without. Keep us safe from the evil one with all his subtlety and with all his skill. Keep us safe from evil people. Keep our lips from speaking evil, be it foul or destructive. Deliver us from thinking evil, dwelling on evil, doing evil.'

References

Wrestling with mighty spiritual forces – Ephesians 6:12
Satan behind Job's temptation to curse God - Job 1:9-11
Satan behind Peter's fall - Luke 22:31-34
Satan behind the temptations of our Lord - Matthew 4:1-11
'In quietness and confidence' - Isaiah 30:15
Warning to Peter - Luke 22:39-46
God looks on the heart - 1 Samuel 16:7

Questions

1   To what extent does Satan keep in the shadows?

2   Why do moral values that are not anchored to godliness drift? What anchor has God our Father given us?

3   Why will true disciples appear increasingly 'odd' in an ungodly society?

4   Why might it encourage us to know that the ancient Roman Empire was the seed bed of the Christian church?

5   In what ways does ungodly thinking undermine the family? Are there costs, of different kinds, to the children, wider family, community and state?

6   In what way have you seen Satan play the secret destroyer among disciples in the church?

7 Do we need to be personally watchful? For what kind of things, situations and people?

8 How can evil creep up on us until we are all but spiritually dead, or at least fruitless?

9 Do we need to be aware and praying much more for one another: that we may recognise and resist Satan's fiery darts?

10 In what ways might we play into Satan's hands?

11 How will the fact that true disciples are caught up in spiritual warfare affect the way in which we live?

12 'No hidden secrets or double agents' - Why is it so hard to openly confess? What encouragement is there to do so?